THE GOOD, THE BAD, AND THE UGLY
BUFFALO BILLS

THE GOOD, THE BAD, AND THE UGLY
BUFFALO BILLS

HEART-POUNDING, JAW-DROPPING, AND GUT-WRENCHING
MOMENTS FROM BUFFALO BILLS HISTORY

Scott Pitoniak

TRIUMPH
BOOKS

Library of Congress Cataloging-in-Publication Data

Pitoniak, Scott.
    The good, the bad, and the ugly Buffalo Bills : heart-pounding, jaw-dropping, and gut-wrenching moments from Buffalo Bills history / Scott Pitoniak.
    p. cm.
    ISBN-13: 978-1-60078-008-0
    ISBN-10: 1-60078-008-3
    1. Buffalo Bills (Football team)—History. I. Title.

GV956.B83P583 2007
796.332'640974797—dc22

                                                    2007018181

This book is available in quantity at special discounts for your group or organization. For further information, contact:

Triumph Books
542 South Dearborn Street
Suite 750
Chicago, Illinois 60605
(312) 939-3330
Fax (312) 663-3557

Printed in U.S.A.
ISBN: 978-1-60078-008-0
Design by Patricia Frey
All photos courtesy of AP/Wide World Photos unless otherwise indicated.

To the Loves of My Life—
Beth, Amy, and Christopher

CONTENTS

PREFACE

When I was assigned to the Buffalo Bills' beat back in 1985, several colleagues offered condolences. I quickly discovered why.

Those were the bad old days of back-to-back 2–14 seasons; of home games with 60,000 fans disguised as empty seats; of coaches who turned clichés into malapropisms; of bumper stickers that read: BRING PROFESSIONAL FOOTBALL BACK TO WESTERN NEW YORK.

Things were so bad that during a mini-camp visit to a suburban Rochester, New York, high school in the spring of '86, Bills owner Ralph Wilson hinted the franchise might run a down-and-out-of-town. To Jacksonville. Or Baltimore. Or Nashville. Or some other football-starved burg that didn't have a National Football League franchise at the time. Just over 19,000 season tickets wasn't going to cut it anymore, warned the man who paid the bills.

And then on a breezy August day two weeks before the '86 regular-season opener, the United States Football League went belly-up, Jim Kelly became available, and everything changed. The swaggering quarterback whom *Sports Illustrated* called "Namath with knees" was coming to the city he had been dissing ever since Buffalo selected him in the first round of the 1983 draft.

Faster than you could say "Machine Gun Kelly," the Bills became the hottest ticket in western New York, not to mention a plum assignment for a sportswriter.

The 20 years that followed would be quite a roller-coaster ride, a time for Bills fans to shout and pout. We would witness an incredible football renaissance sparked not only by Kelly, but by people such as Wilson, Marv Levy, Bill Polian, Thurman Thomas, Bruce Smith, Andre Reed, and Steve Tasker. We would chronicle the ecstasy of a 51–3 rout of the Raiders in the 1990 AFC title game, as well as the greatest comeback in pro football history. And we would also report on the agony of "wide right," the four Super Bowl losses, and the demotion of O.J. Simpson from American hero to social pariah.

We would watch the rivalry with the Dolphins finally swing in Buffalo's favor after the Bills went zero-for-the-decade in the 1970s against the hated Fish.

We would witness another resurrection of the franchise in the late 1990s, as Doug Flutie became so popular that they named a cereal after him. But Flutie's legendary status in Buffalo would be short-lived: he and Rob Johnson became embroiled in a nasty quarterback controversy that made the quarterback duel of the mid-1960s between Jack Kemp and Daryle Lamonica seem calm by comparison.

Along the way, we would learn about the incredible passion western New Yorkers have for their football team—a passion underscored by the fact that the Bills led the league in attendance for six consecutive seasons despite playing in the NFL's third-smallest market.

We touch on all of this and more in *The Good, the Bad, and the Ugly: Buffalo Bills*. While it doesn't profess to be the definitive history of the franchise, it does attempt to highlight the people and moments that have made the Bills a family tradition passed down from one generation to the next.

As Van Miller, the legendary voice of the Bills, used to say before opening kickoffs: "Fasten your seat belts, folks." We hope you enjoy the ride back in time.

Cheers.

—Scott Pitoniak
February 28, 2007

ACKNOWLEDGMENTS

The author would like to thank Bob Snodgrass and the staff at Triumph Books for making this project a reality.

He also would like to thank the following people and organizations for their input and support: Ed Abramoski, Beth Adams, Rick Azar, Scott Berchtold, Frank Bilovsky, Jay Bonfatti, Russ Brandon, the Buffalo Bills, Lary Bump, Vic Carucci, Mark Dalton, Bob Dicesare, Mike Doser, Donn Esmonde, Larry Felser, Mark Gaughan, Jim Gehman, Jamie Germano, Bucky Gleason, Ted Haider, Mike Haim, Blythe Hurley, Chris Jenkins, Jim Kelley, Marv Levy, Denny Lynch, Sal Maiorana, Bob Matthews, Van Miller, John Murphy, Milt Northrop, Amy Pitoniak, Christopher Pitoniak, Chuck Pollock, Amy Reagan, the *Rochester Democrat and Chronicle*, Leo Roth, Dave Senko, Jerry Sullivan, Steve Tasker, L. Budd Thalman, Ellen Vinz, John Wawrow, and Allen Wilson.

The following publications and wire services were invaluable during the research for and writing of this book: the *Rochester Democrat and Chronicle*; the *Rochester Times-Union*; *The Buffalo News*; the *Buffalo Courier-Express*; *USA Today*; the *Olean Times Herald*; *The New York Times*; *Sports Illustrated*; *The Sporting News*; *The Boston Globe*; *The Tennessean*; *The Buffalo Bills Media Guide* (1960–2006); *Sport* magazine; *Inside Sports*; The Associated Press; United Press International; Buffalobills.com; NFL.com; *Relentless: The Hard-Hitting History of Buffalo Bills Football* by Sal

Maiorana; *Relentless II: The Hard-Hitting History of Buffalo Bills Football* by Sal Maiorana; *The Buffalo Bills Official Trivia Book* by Scott Pitoniak; and *The Buffalo Bills All-New Trivia Book* by Scott Pitoniak.

INTRODUCTION

It was supposed to be Miami, not Buffalo. It was supposed to be the city Bills fans have grown to despise, home of the hated Dolphins.

That's where Ralph Wilson's heart, wallet, and football compass originally pointed. That's where he wanted to set up shop back in 1960.

"I was all set to go there, but the University of Miami wouldn't lease the Orange Bowl to me," he recalled. "Miami had had bad luck with new football teams. They had a team in the old All-American Football Conference after World War II. I think it folded around the third quarter of its seventh game. The last thing they wanted was another pro team that might not be able to pay its rent."

Wilson returned home to Detroit, disappointed that his dream of owning a professional football team had died. But a few days later, Lamar Hunt, one of the men trying to launch the American Football League, called to say the circuit desperately needed an eighth team to balance its schedule. He gave Wilson a list of prospective cities that also included St. Louis, Louisville, Cincinnati, and Buffalo.

Wilson asked a sportswriter he knew in Detroit this question: "If you were dumb enough to go into a new football league and you had these five cities to choose from, which one would you pick?"

Without hesitation, the writer answered: "Buffalo."

> "WE DIDN'T HAVE ANY SCOUTING DEPARTMENT [IN 1960]. HECK, WE ONLY HAD FOUR COACHES, SO YOU HAD TO WEAR A LOT OF HATS. WE DRAFTED PLAYERS, BUT I ALSO CALLED AROUND TO A LOT OF MY FRIENDS WHO WERE COLLEGE COACHES TO GET THE WORD OUT. YOU LITERALLY HAD GUYS COMING IN OFF THE STREET WHO HAD NO BUSINESS BEING THERE."
>
> —COACH BUSTER RAMSEY ON BUILDING THE FIRST BILLS TEAM

So Wilson flew to Buffalo and toured the city with Paul Neville, the managing editor of *The Buffalo Evening News*.

"We had lunch and he said, 'Geez, we'd really like to have you put your franchise here,'" Wilson recalled. "I said, 'OK, Paul, here's what I'll do. If your paper will support me for three years, I'll put the franchise here.'"

The men shook hands. Wilson gave the league a one-in-10 chance of surviving against the established NFL.

"They weren't good odds, but I had always been a risk-taker in business. I really believe in going for it on fourth-and-one," he said.

The skeptics said Wilson and the other original AFL owners were card-carrying members of the "foolish club" because only an idiot would plunk down a $25,000 franchise fee and be silly enough to believe they could play ball with the big, bad National Football League. But the Bills and their AFL brethren proved their worth, eventually landing a huge network television contract and forcing a merger with the established NFL in 1966.

There have been several occasions along the way when the Bills octogenarian owner could have bolted for greener—as in the color of money—pastures, but Wilson stuck it out. And he's glad he did.

"The people here have endured some tough economic times, but they've done a great job supporting the Bills, under the circumstances," he said. "The team has given them and me a lot to cheer about through the years."

His Detroit-based company, Wilson Enterprises, has dabbled in everything from highway construction to ownership of several television stations. Along the way, Wilson, an avid horseman, has bred two thoroughbreds that raced in the Kentucky Derby. But none of his businesses have provided him with the thrill or the exposure that the Bills have.

> **"I SWEAR, HE KEPT THIS ONE GUY ON THE TEAM BECAUSE HE COULD PLAY THE HARMONICA."**
>
> —TRAINER EDDIE ABRAMOSKI ON BUSTER RAMSEY, WHO OCCASIONALLY LED HIS PLAYERS IN SONG ON PLANE TRIPS

Wilson had an inkling early on that he would eventually become involved in professional football. He recalls attending Detroit Lions games with his father, and he once owned some stock in the team.

Wilson is pleased he hung in there during the difficult early years of the AFL. "I never thought about throwing in the towel, but there were times when I did remind myself that I used to pay $5 for a ticket to a Lions game and I enjoyed myself and had no headaches," he said with the laughter of a man thrilled by tackling challenges. "I would ask myself what I was doing here."

By January 1965, he had stopped asking himself that question. Wilson's Bills were coming off their first AFL title at the time, and he had joined the late Baltimore Colts owner Carroll Rosenbloom for talks about the possibility of a merger with the NFL.

"The thing that had made us players was the network television contract we had landed," Wilson said. "I think that gave us legitimacy, and I think the NFL had made the cardinal business mistake by underestimating the competition. They became complacent."

> **"THERE WERE WOODS AT THE END OF THE PRACTICE FIELD, AND OL' BUSTER TOLD ALL OF US TO RUN INTO THEM. THE GUYS WHO DODGED THE TREES BECAME RUNNING BACKS AND RECEIVERS AND THE GUYS WHO RAN INTO THE TREES BECAME LINEMEN."**
>
> —RECEIVER TOM RYCHLEC ON HOW COACH RAMSEY DECIDED WHO WOULD PLAY WHERE

> "YOU COULDN'T BLAME PEOPLE FOR THINKING MR. WILSON AND THE
> OTHER AFL OWNERS WERE FOOLS. PEOPLE IN THE NFL LOOKED DOWN
> ON US LIKE WE WERE A BUNCH OF BUSH LEAGUERS, WHICH WE PROBABLY
> WERE AT THE START. BUT THAT CHANGED IN TIME, AND IT LOOKS LIKE
> MR. WILSON AND THOSE OTHER OLD AFL GUYS GOT THE LAST LAUGH."
>
> —BUSTER RAMSEY

Through the years, Wilson endured his share of criticism from Bills fans and the media who covered the team. He was called cheap, and people said he didn't care as much about fielding a contending club because he was an absentee owner who lived in Detroit.

But the public perception finally turned positive during the late 1980s and early '90s, when Buffalonians began to realize that Wilson was deeply committed to winning a Super Bowl and, more importantly, to keeping the franchise in western New York.

"People used to throw their programs at me," he liked to joke. "Now, they're asking me to sign them."

Wilson has always enjoyed a hearty laugh, and he has never minded laughing at himself. He told a story once about how a friend urged him to deliver a pep talk to the Bills after they had fallen behind 21–7 at the half. "I gave an inspirational five-minute speech that would have made Vince Lombardi and Knute Rockne proud. The final score was 51–7, and my friend says to me, 'Wilson, you talked to the wrong team.'"

As he closes in on his 90th birthday, Wilson continues to battle for an equitable revenue-sharing system that will ensure the long-term viability of small-market franchises like Buffalo. Some longtime football observers have called him "the conscience of the NFL" because, unlike large-market owners such as Jerry Jones and Daniel Snyder, he realizes that the ability of all teams to be competitive is what helped make the league enormously successful in the first place.

"I think people like the fact that we've had competitive balance through the years," he said. "People like to know that an underdog market like a Green Bay or a Buffalo or a Cleveland can compete with the Washington Redskins and New York Giants and Chicago Bears. I'd hate to see the day come when that's not the case."

It's always bothered him to see franchises up and leave. In fact, he was one of just two owners to vote against the Cleveland Browns' move to Baltimore in the 1990s. During the lean years with the Bills—and there have been several—Wilson was courted by other cities to pull up stakes. But he stayed put. And he doesn't regret the decision, even though it cost him millions.

Not that the Bills haven't been a great investment: a national business publication recently valued Wilson's team at more than half a billion dollars.

Some fool, huh?

And to think, this love affair between owner, team, and region never would have taken place had the city of Miami not told Wilson to take a hike nearly a half-century ago.

As he prepared for his 48th season, Wilson was asked how he would like to be remembered by Buffalo fans. There was a long pause.

> "THEY USED TO THROW THEIR GAME PROGRAMS AT ME. NOW, THEY ARE ASKING ME TO SIGN THEM."
>
> —RALPH WILSON

"There are a lot of people who go through life who don't do anything for anybody," he said. "They're born. They live. They're gone. I believe people should make some sort of contribution to make the world better. It doesn't have to be major. It can be minor. I would like to think that by bringing the Bills to western New York, I've made a contribution to improving the quality of life here. That's how I would like to be remembered."

THE GOOD, THE BAD, AND THE UGLY
BUFFALO BILLS

THE GOOD

MARVELOUS MARV

When Marv Levy was hired to replace Hank Bullough midway through the 1986 season, many believed the new Buffalo Bills coach would wind up being a bust rather than receiving one.

The smart money was on his NFL career dying in the coaches' graveyard that was Buffalo rather than him being immortalized with pro football legends such as Lombardi and Shula in Canton, Ohio.

Not only was Levy walking into what seemed like a hopeless situation—the Bills had won just six of their previous 43 games—but he was coming to town with an uninspiring head coaching resume that included a 31–42 record in five seasons with the Kansas City Chiefs.

The fact that Levy was 61 at the time only added to the belief that he would be nothing more than an interim coach, destined to follow in the forgettable footsteps of Bullough, Kay Stephenson, and Harvey Johnson.

"There was a lot of skepticism on the part of the fans and the media, and I understood that because I had made some coaching decisions in the past that you might say didn't exactly work out," said Bills owner Ralph Wilson, chuckling. "But I had a strong feeling things would be different under Marv. He was a very, very impressive person, extremely intelligent. He had a great knowledge

MARVISMS

Marv Levy's bromides struck a chord with players and fans. Here are some of the coach's more memorable sayings.

On taking risks: "If Michelangelo wanted to play it safe, he would have painted the floor of the Sistine Chapel."

On keeping things in perspective: "World War II was a must-win."

Addressing his team after having surgery to remove his cancerous prostate: "My heart and soul will be with you, but my prostate won't."

Levy's signature phrase before each game: "Where would you rather be than right here, right now?"

On Bills general manager and longtime friend Bill Polian: "He is more aware of what's going on around him than a smoke detector."

On the coach-fan relationship: "The coach that starts listening to the fans winds up sitting next to them."

On an aging quarterback's quickness: "He hasn't lost any speed—he never had any."

On going the extra mile: "You have to add 'tri' to your 'umph' if you want to triumph."

On how coaches feel about change: "When it comes to coaches, *change* is a six-letter word. It leads to a five-letter word—*chaos*—which results in a lot of four-letter words, and none of them are nice."

of the game of football and a great sense of humor. I just had this intuition that he would be the perfect person to turn things around. I really believed he would hit a home run for us."

Try a grand slam.

Levy, who was inducted into the Pro Football Hall of Fame in 2001, fit the Bills perfectly. Under his guidance, they won six division titles and four conference championships, led the NFL in attendance six consecutive seasons, and made it to the Super Bowl an unprecedented four straight times.

And although they lost each of those Bowl games, they earned the respect of the sports world for their ability to bounce back from disappointment season after season after season.

The source of their resiliency was no secret. It came from Levy, who staged a remarkable comeback from prostate cancer surgery.

"I think you take on the personality of your head coach, and we took on Marv's," said Jim Kelly, the quarterback of those great Bills teams. "He taught us it was OK to mourn those losses for awhile, but then it was time to pick yourself up and move on."

There were many lessons Levy provided. His use of words as big as former offensive tackle Howard "House" Ballard resulted in furrowed brows and sent players and reporters scrambling for dictionaries.

"My vocabulary improved tenfold playing for Marv," center Kent Hull once joked. "There was a whole lot of head-shaking going on when Marv used those ten-dollar words you've never heard of. Heck, for all I knew he could have been making those words up."

Levy, who was big on war analogies, once alluded to the German army's overconfidence during World War II and the importance of "crossing one river at a time, like Hannibal."

"To be honest," Levy replied when asked about the metaphor, "I don't know how many of these guys even knew what World War II was, and they probably think Hannibal is an offensive tackle for the Jets."

> **"IT'S SO GREAT TO FINALLY HAVE SOMETHING TO CELEBRATE ON A SUPER BOWL WEEKEND."**
>
> —MARV LEVY UPON LEARNING THAT HE HAD BEEN VOTED INTO THE PRO FOOTBALL HALL OF FAME ON JANUARY 27, 2001

They probably didn't know much about their coach's history either. But had they done some research on Levy, they would have discovered the embodiment of the American dream. The son of Jewish immigrants who came to America from England at the dawn of the 20th century, Marvin Daniel Levy grew up on Chicago's south side. His father, Sam Levy, ran a produce market and instilled in Marv the importance of a strong work ethic and a good sense of humor. From his mother, Ida Levy, Marv developed a love for literature and history.

Sam Levy established himself as the Windy City's top high school basketball player in the early 1900s, but his dreams of

Despite an uninspiring record in Kansas City and low expectations from most Buffalo fans, Marv Levy was perfect for the Bills, winning six division titles, four conference championships, and an unprecedented four straight trips to the Super Bowl.

college were dashed when he was drafted by the army to fight in World War I.

Marv inherited his father's athletic genes and wound up excelling in football and track in high school and at Coe College in Iowa. He also excelled in the classroom, earning his Phi Beta Kappa key and admission to Harvard Law School. But after a month at Harvard, Levy realized he had no desire to become an attorney. His heart was in teaching and coaching. He transferred to Harvard's graduate school, where he earned a degree in English history. From there, he landed a job at St. Louis Country Day School in Missouri, where he began a coaching odyssey that would last 47 years.

Along the way, he would coach football at Coe College, the University of New Mexico, the University of California (Berkeley), and the College of William & Mary.

Levy's first NFL job came in 1969 as an assistant with the Philadelphia Eagles. A year later, George Allen hired him as the special-teams coach of the Los Angeles Rams. His years under Allen in L.A. and with the Washington Redskins would further shape his coaching philosophy.

After the Redskins lost the Super Bowl in January 1973, Levy took the head-coaching job with the Montreal Alouettes of the Canadian Football League and led them to two Grey Cup titles in five years.

His success caught the attention of Chiefs owner Lamar Hunt, who hired him to resuscitate a Kansas City team that had been 2–12 in 1977. Slowly but surely, Levy turned things around there, improving the Chiefs to 9–7 by 1981. But the NFL players' strike the following year tore the team asunder, and Levy was fired. At the time, Chuck Knox was leaving Buffalo to take a job as head coach with the Seattle Seahawks, and Levy interviewed for the Bills vacancy. Marv had an excellent interview, but Wilson opted instead to promote Bills offensive coordinator Kay Stephenson.

"I was extremely impressed with Marv then, but I thought I owed it to Kay," Wilson said. "It was one of those 51–49 decisions. Nothing against Kay, but in retrospect, I made the wrong decision. I should have hired Marv then and there."

After a year with the Chicago Blitz of the now-defunct United States Football League and a year out of football, Levy headed back to Montreal to become the Alouettes' director of football operations in 1986.

"I didn't know if I would ever get another opportunity to coach in the NFL," he said. "I knew it would be a long shot."

Wilson replaced Stephenson with Hank Bullough four games into the 1985 season, but the losing continued—even after Jim Kelly joined the roster before the 1986 season kicked off. After the Bills stumbled to a 2–7 start in Bullough's first full season, Wilson found himself in the market for yet another head coach.

"I finally got it right in 1986," Wilson said. "When I was thinking about replacing Hank, I called Lamar to see what he felt about Marv. He said, 'Ralph, I never should have fired him.' That was good enough for me."

Levy couldn't believe his good fortune.

"I was licking my chops because I saw Buffalo as a sleeping giant," he said. "Talk about being a lucky guy. I walk into my first meeting and there's a young Jim Kelly and a young Bruce Smith and a young Andre Reed. Much of the puzzle was already constructed by the time I arrived. And I had a general manager [Bill Polian] who was an astute judge of talent and an owner who was hungry and committed to winning. If we avoided catastrophic injuries, I believed we could turn it around in a hurry."

And they did.

"HE TOOK A STRUGGLING FRANCHISE—THE BOAT WAS REALLY ROCKING—AND HE RIGHTED THE SHIP. THIS GENTLEMAN HAD GREAT PLAYERS. BUT I KNOW ORGANIZATIONS THAT HAVE GREAT PLAYERS AND THEY NEVER MAKE THE PLAYOFFS. IF YOU DON'T HAVE A GREAT LEADER, YOU CAN HAVE ALL THE GREAT PLAYERS IN THE WORLD AND YOU WON'T WIN."

—RALPH WILSON ON MARV LEVY'S INDUCTION TO THE PRO FOOTBALL HALL OF FAME

MARV'S LITTLE WHITE LIE

Fearing he might not get another shot at being a head coach if he told the truth, Marv Levy fudged his age a bit before joining the Bills in the middle of the 1986 season. Nothing major, mind you. He just said he was 58 rather than 61. Levy's cover was blown in 1995, when a computer check of licenses issued by the New York State Department of Motor Vehicles revealed his real date of birth as August 3, 1925. That meant he was 70 rather than 67 at the time. Not that it ever mattered, because Levy's mind and body have always been much younger than his chronological age. Toward the end of his coaching career, the truth wound up working in his favor. By coaching at age 72, he was able to tie George "Papa Bear" Halas as the oldest man to coach an NFL team.

Thanks to shrewd trades and drafting, which added the likes of Cornelius Bennett, Thurman Thomas, and Shane Conlan, the Bills reached the AFC Championship Game by Levy's second full season. By his fourth full season, they were in Super Bowl XXV, where they lost a heartbreaking 20–19 decision after Scott Norwood's 47-yard field-goal attempt sailed wide right.

Three consecutive Super Bowl defeats would follow.

"I would have loved to have won at least one of them, but life goes on," Levy said. "The last thing I want my players to feel is that their careers were somehow less significant because they didn't win a Super Bowl. There is something to be said for making it that close to the summit of the mountain four straight times."

His corny, self-deprecating sense of humor, along with his sense of fairness and the courage he displayed while missing three games to have his cancerous prostate removed, endeared him to players, coaches, reporters, fans, and club executives. His ability to laugh at himself and with others helped him flourish in a profession that often devours its practitioners.

Levy loved to tell jokes at team meetings. He often quoted Churchill or Roosevelt or some other historical figure.

"ONE TIME WE WERE PLAYING A TEAM THAT WAS A HEAVY FAVORITE. THEY WERE BEING PORTRAYED AS A BUNCH OF SUPERMEN. I SAID TO OUR GUYS, 'HEY, NOT TO WORRY. WE ONCE CUT SUPERMAN.'"

—MARV LEVY, REFERRING TO DEAN CAIN, WHO PLAYED SUPERMAN ON TELEVISION SEVERAL YEARS AFTER BEING RELEASED IN TRAINING CAMP BY THE BILLS

"There is a method to his madness," Thomas said during one of Levy's final seasons as coach. "He does and says things for a reason. When you really think about what he says you see how it pertains to what the team or you are going through. He's not just book-smart; he's people-smart."

He obviously was football-smart, too. Levy's teams went 123–78 and won six divisional titles and four conference titles. Twice, Levy was named NFL Coach of the Year. He coached the Bills until age 72, tying him with Chicago legend "Papa Bear" George Halas for the record as the oldest coach in league history.

When he retired following the 1997 season, he wrote his memoirs and worked as a network television football analyst. Though he itched to coach again, no one would give him a shot because they believed he was too old.

After the Bills' meltdown under General Manager Tom Donahoe and Head Coach Mike Mularkey during the 2005 season, Wilson was looking to shake things up. He asked his old friend Levy if he would be interested in returning to the team as general manager, and Marv jumped at the opportunity. The in-with-the-old, out-with-the-new approach initially was criticized, but it started to look brilliant as the season progressed.

At the ripe old age of 80, Levy pumped new life into the franchise by hiring a head coach who was similar to him in many ways. Ivy League–educated Dick Jauron brought a sense of organization and confidence to the team, and helped J.P. Losman develop into a stable quarterback. Though they finished just 7–9, the Bills were in playoff contention until the final two weeks of the regular season.

Wilson couldn't be more pleased with the job Levy has done.

"I've had some coaches here who treated me as if they owned the team," he said. "They didn't want me around; they acted like Julius Caesar. Marv's not that way at all. He is a man of great humility, not one of those big-me, little-you kind of guys. He has a great sense of humor, great intellect, and a wonderful way with people."

Those who wondered if Levy would be up to the demanding task at his age have been silenced. Levy remains in remarkable shape. He occasionally cites studies at USC and Tufts that indicate work is the best way to ward off the deleterious effects of aging. "Hell, Marv's in better shape than half the players in the league," Thomas said. "His mind's as sharp as it was when I first met him. He seems to be as driven and motivated as he's ever been."

The history buff also can find plenty of historical precedence for not placing age-related restrictions on people. Levy could talk about how Albert Schweitzer was running a hospital at age 89. Or how Michelangelo was still painting at 88. Or how Benjamin Franklin helped write the United States Constitution at 81. Or how George Burns was still making 'em laugh at 100.

Marv Levy's Hall of Fame Acceptance Speech

For as long as he can remember, Marv Levy has admired Winston Churchill. He loved listening to old broadcasts of the late British prime minister's speeches. He was always inspired by the beauty of Churchill's words, the power of his message. "To me, he is the greatest orator that I've been able to identify," Levy said. "I think he was the most prominent historical figure of the 20th century. He was rarely wrong. All through the 1930s, he was warning us about Hitler and he was considered a voice in the wilderness. He rallied a totally defeated people in World War II. He made a great

---

"THE ONLY THING I KNOW ABOUT ROLLING STONES IS THEY GATHER NO MOSS."

—MARV LEVY, WHEN ASKED ABOUT THE ROLLING STONES BEFORE
AN APPEARANCE BY THE WORLD-FAMOUS ROCK BAND AT RICH STADIUM

"I'M VERY PROUD TO BRING SOME YOUTH TO THIS ORGANIZATION."

—87-YEAR-OLD RALPH WILSON AT THE PRESS CONFERENCE ANNOUNCING
THE RETURN OF 80-YEAR-OLD MARV LEVY AS THE BILLS' GENERAL MANAGER

---

statement at the end of the war when he said, 'It was the British people who had the heart of a lion. I was fortunate enough to provide the roar.' And he did."

For 12 years, Levy provided the roar for the Buffalo Bills. And on Saturday, August 4, 2001, on the sunburned steps of the Pro Football Hall of Fame in Canton, Ohio, the winningest coach in franchise history provided it again with Churchill-like impact and eloquence. In accepting induction into football's most exclusive fraternity, Levy delivered a speech his idol surely would have enjoyed—a speech full of wit, wisdom, and just the right touch of humor. In 14½ minutes, he hit on the high points of an extraordinary journey and the people who made it possible. To paraphrase Churchill, this very well may have been Levy's finest hour. Here's Marv's speech from that historic day.

Thank you very much. Thank you.

It's been a long trip from the corner of 71st Street and Stony Island Avenue on the south side of Chicago to Canton, Ohio. It's taken me 76 years. But in the words of an old song, I wouldn't have missed it for the world, because on every step of this joyous journey, I've been accompanied by some remarkable companions.

Many of them are here today, and although there are others who are unable to be here, I'll always know exactly where to find every one of you—right here in my heart forever.

The Pro Football Hall of Fame is a hallowed institution, and I feel some indescribable emotions today upon becoming an inductee along with these six other men who've contributed so much to the game we all revere. Our welcome in Canton by everyone here has been overwhelming. Thank you for making this such a memorable day in my life. I'm grateful to the Hall of Fame board of selectors, those respected members of the national media—including Buffalo's Larry Felser—for allowing me to join the company of those who have entered this hall before me.

When I first walked out onto the practice field as a high school assistant football coach exactly a half-century ago next month, men like Jim Thorpe, Bronko Nagurski, Sid Luckman, and Marion Motley were mythical gods. They still are, and I tread this ground with great reverence for them and for all who reside here. Never did I dream that someday I might be invited to share these same lodgings with them.

How could it happen? Well, it's because of some wondrous people, without whose love, abilities, and counsel I'd not be standing here today. My father Sam, by his lifelong example, displayed for me the virtues of an honest day's work and of great personal courage.

You as avid football fans undoubtedly have witnessed many exciting runs from scrimmage. But the greatest run I ever knew of was by my father, who during World War I, along with his comrades from the storied Fourth Marine Brigade, raced several hundred yards into withering machine-gun fire, across the wheat fields at Belleau Wood in France. Their valor on that June day in 1918 succeeded in halting the German army advance just 25 miles from Paris.

MASTERING THE "DON" OF NFL COACHES

Good thing Don Shula didn't have to coach every game against Marv Levy or he'd never have made it to the top of the NFL's all-time coaching victory list. Levy's Bills held a decided edge against Shula's Dolphins during the late '80s and early '90s, winning 17 of the 22 meetings between the two Hall of Fame coaches.

HANKISMS

If Marv Levy was the Bills' bard, then Hank Bullough was its buffoon. During his one and a half seasons in Buffalo, the man who preceded Levy as head coach waged a losing battle against NFL opponents and the mother tongue.

Bullough's teams won only four of 21 games before he was fired on November 3, 1986. His record with the English language was even worse.

Like Yogi Berra and George W. Bush, Bullough unintentionally entertained people with humorous malaprops. He often praised his team's "work ethnic" and talked about making decisions on the "spare of the moment." After a loss to the New York Jets, he said a long pass play had taken "the sails right out of our wind."

Here's a look at some other memorable Bullough-props.

On his team's progress: "We keep beating ourselves, but we're getting better at it."

On interference from owner Ralph Wilson: "I'm not a yes guy. He knew that when I hired him."

On a question from a belligerent caller to his radio show about the length of his contract: "I don't wish to indulge that information."

On a question about whether Jim Kelly's multimillion-dollar contract was insured: "You mean with Lords of London."

On the Bills' plans in a college draft that featured Bo Jackson and Napoleon McCallum: "Well, you've got that Jackson kid at Auburn and that Napoleon Bonaparte kid at Navy."

On playing well but losing: "I don't believe in morale victories."

On the lack of response to filling a vacancy on his staff: "I haven't exactly been divulged with phone calls."

On the development of one of his quarterbacks: "He's making improvement throwing the ball where he's throwing the ball."

He was my hero even before I was born. One day many years later I telephoned my father to tell him I was leaving Harvard Law School and that I wanted to be a football coach.

Thirty seconds of painful silence followed, and then the old Marine said simply, "Be a good one!"

I hope I haven't disappointed him.

My dear mother Ida enjoyed more peaceful pursuits, and although she never went beyond first grade in elementary school, she'd read the complete works of Shakespeare and countless others. And from her I acquired an appreciation of literature and of the worthy deeds which great literature inspires. Both Sam and Ida have been gone for many years now, but I feel their presence with me here today. And because of them I have my sweet sister Marilyn, who is indeed here to share this occasion with me. In her you'll find the best qualities of our parents. Lucky lady.

Today, fond memories are flashing through my mind. I still recall the fearsome exhortations—look it up, Thurman—of my high school coach, Nate Wasserman, and another great Chicago high school coach, Joe Kupcinet. I remember my teammates at South Shore High School, and I remember with pride those 21 classmates whom I joined when we all enlisted in the Army Air Corps on the day after we graduated high school in 1943.

"Nothing can stop the Army Air Corps!" I told you I'd sing up here, fellas.

Nineteen of us came home after the war. The other three remain forever young. Two close friends from my high school days are here today—Herb Melnick and Nick Kladis. What great friends!

I remember my teammates at Coe College, and I remember with affection my college football coach, Dick Clausen. He showed me what a noble profession coaching can be. It was my privilege to play for Dick Clausen and later to serve on his staff at my alma mater and then at the University of New Mexico, where I got to coach Don Perkins, who became the first in that string of great Dallas Cowboys running backs. I remember fondly the warmhearted eloquence of a brilliant educator, Davis Y. Paschall, president of the College of William & Mary.

As a head coach in professional football, I've worked with three different owners, men of impeccable integrity. First was Sam Berger of the Montreal Alouettes in the Canadian Football League. The two Grey Cup championships I shared with that distinguished gentleman, with those superb players and uplifting fans in Montreal, leave me with treasured memories. Merci, mon ami.

In 1978 Lamar Hunt, an NFL legend, hired me to coach the Kansas City Chiefs and players like Tom Condon, Fuzzy Kremer, and Joe Delaney. I will always value my association with Lamar and the fine people in Kansas City.

And then there is Buffalo's Ralph Wilson. I worked for him for 12 glorious years. But he wasn't my boss. He was my friend, and he remains my friend. His contributions to this game are unbounded. He deserves to be enshrined here in Canton, and may that day come soon.

The rookie general manager who brought this then-out-of-work 61-year-old coach 18 years his senior to Buffalo was Bill Polian, who honors me by being my presenter today. Together Bill and I decided to employ some obscure USFL scout as our director of player personnel. His name was John Butler.

Bill Polian and John Butler, the two best general managers in football. Smart, honest, witty, energetic, astute, and incredibly capable. To them and to personnel directors Bob Ferguson, A.J. Smith, Dwight Adams, Norm Pollom, and their excellent staff of scouts, I am indebted for that parade of talented, high-character players whom I am so proud to have coached.

I sure didn't coach them alone. How fortunate I was to work with the men who served on our coaching staff, several of whom are here today—Tom Bresnahan, Bruce DeHaven, Don Lawrence, Dick Roach, Dan Sekanovich, and Elijah Pitts's widow, lovely Ruth. So is Ed Abramoski,

Marv Levy flashes a smile while he poses with his bronze bust after his enshrinement into the Pro Football Hall of Fame in Canton, Ohio, in August 2001.

who was the Bills' head trainer for more than 30 years. Along with coaches like Ted Marchibroda, Walt Corey, Ted Cottrell, Charlie Joiner, Chuck Lester, Rusty Jones, Jim Shofner, and Dan Henning, they are all representative of a coaching staff that is unparalleled. Our secretaries, Nina and Nancy, that includes you.

I will never forget that first time I walked into the Buffalo Bills' team meeting room in early November of 1986 upon being appointed in midseason to take over as head coach. Sitting in that room were a young Jim Kelly, Andre Reed, Bruce Smith, Kent Hull, and Darryl Talley: great leaders. So were Jim Ritcher, Pete Metzelaars, Will Wolford, Dwight Drane, Fred Smerlas, Mark Kelso, and

Mark Pike. Soon to join them: Steve Tasker, Shane Conlan, Cornelius Bennett—thank you, Bill, for that trade, by the way—Howard Ballard, Thurman Thomas—thank you, John Butler—Kenny Davis, Henry Jones, Phil Hansen, and speedy receivers like Don Beebe and James Lofton. Each of those guys could run the minute in 57 seconds, time 'em.

Then came Glenn Parker, John Fina, Chris Mohr, Steve Christie, Chris Spielman—thank you Ohio State University and Canton. How lucky can a man get?

What an odyssey I lived with those men, with their teammates and coaches, with all the wonderful people in the Bills organization, and with those incomparable Buffalo Bills fans. For six consecutive years they led the NFL in attendance. Who cared if it was bitter cold or if an angry snowstorm was raging? Their spirits were as tough as linebackers; their hearts were as warm as the thermal underwear I wore during those January playoff games in Orchard Park. And what about those great players and coaches against whom we competed so fiercely? I'm so proud to have walked the opposite sideline from Hall of Fame coaches Don Shula, Tom Landry, Bill Walsh, Bud Grant, Chuck Noll, and Joe Gibbs. And to have walked the same sideline as an assistant to a coach from whom I learned so much and to whom I owe so much, the inimitable George Allen.

Then there are those who are closest to me who sustained and encouraged me, even during moments of searing disappointment. My precious wife Frannie—the happiest when we won, the saddest when we lost, the quickest to shed a tear or to wipe away one of mine. She has brought me love and joy, and, like her, a beautiful daughter—my darling daughter Kimberly, who arrived here just last night from Europe so that she could share this day with me. You coaches out there, may all your players have Kimberly's energy and her spirit and be as devoted as she is. And to my former wife Dorothy, who was with me during my earlier years of coaching, I am indeed grateful for all we share. Frannie, Kimberly, Dorothy, Marilyn: not one of them ever gained a yard or made a tackle. But without their love I wouldn't be here today.

My family, all girls, is here. Someone once lamented that given my enthrallment with this game, it is a shame that I never had a son. Well, he was wrong. He was wrong. Don't tell me I never had a son. I've had thousands of them, of every size, shape, color, faith, and temperament, and I loved them, every one.

And because of them I still hear echoes from those sounds that glorify this game. I hear the cheers of the crowd as Thurman or Andre goes hurtling into the end zone or as Bruce, Bruce, Bruce sacks yet another quarterback.

I hear the grunts and collisions out on the field of play. I hear Jim Kelly calling cadence at the line of scrimmage. I hear Kent Hull's confident Southern drawl as he relays our line-blocking schemes to his teammates up front. I hear the thundering footsteps of young men as they streak down the field to cover a kickoff. No one ever did it better than two men here today, Steve Tasker and Mark Pike.

And even now I hear the distant strains of college fight songs—"Cheer, Cheer for old Notre Dame"; "The Sturdy Golden Bear"; "Roll Alabama"; "Ten Thousand Men of Harvard"; "On, Brave Old Army Team."

And finally, I hear words spoken to me more than 50 years ago by a man whose memory I cherish. He was my basketball coach and my track coach at Coe College. His name was Harris Lamb. And I will conclude my remarks today by repeating for you what he said to me so many years ago:

"To know the game is great. To play the game is greater. But to love the game is the greatest of them all."

Harris, my dear friend, I have truly loved this game, and I love everyone who has shared this passion with me. Thank you all for enriching my life.

2003 YARDS: A FOOTBALL ODYSSEY

When they arrived at training camp in the summer of 1973, Bills guard Reggie McKenzie pulled O.J. Simpson aside and made a bold prediction.

"Juice," McKenzie said excitedly, "this season you are going to accomplish something that no other running back has ever done."

"What's that?" Simpson asked.

"You're gonna rush for two grand."

Simpson thought McKenzie was joking.

"Why not just shoot for Jim Brown's single-season record [1,863 yards]?" Simpson responded. "That might be more realistic."

"Forget Jim Brown," McKenzie said. "We're gonna shoot for the stars. We're gonna go someplace nobody's been before."

On December 16 of that year, during a snowy afternoon on the chewed-up turf of Shea Stadium in New York, Simpson surpassed everyone's expectations, gaining 200 yards to become the first running back in NFL history to break the 2,000-yard barrier. Eric Dickerson and several others have since eclipsed the Juice's 2,003-yard mark, but it remains significant to Simpson and the blockers who became known as the Electric Company.

> "I LOOK AROUND THE LEAGUE AND I SEE BACKS LIKE NORM BULAICH AND LARRY CSONKA GETTING ALL KINDS OF YARDAGE, AND IT HURTS ME BECAUSE I THINK I'M BETTER THAN THEY ARE."
>
> —O.J. SIMPSON, DECEMBER 1971

Says longtime Bills trainer Eddie Abramoski: "It's like Roger Bannister breaking the four-minute-mile barrier. You can't tell me who currently holds the record in the mile, but you can tell me that Bannister was the first. Same with O.J., and he did his in just 14 games. Dickerson [and the others] needed 16."

There were few signs during that preseason that 1973 was going to be anything special, as Simpson suffered a cracked rib and the Bills lost all six exhibition games.

But Lou Saban wasn't concerned. Through shrewd drafting, the coach, who was in his second tour of duty with the Bills, had

THE CENTURY MARK TIMES TWO

O.J. Simpson opened his historic 1973 season with a bang, gaining a then-NFL record 250 yards in a 31–13 win at New England against the Patriots. He broke the 200-yard mark three times that season, and a league-record six times during his career. Interestingly, the Bills lost two of the games in which he surpassed the 200-yard mark, including a 1976 game in which the Detroit Lions beat Buffalo despite a record output of 273 yards by the Juice.

put together a formidable offensive line that included McKenzie and future Hall of Famer Joe DeLamielleure at the guards, Donnie Green and Dave Foley at the tackles, and Bruce Jarvis and backup Mike Montler at center.

His trump card, though, was Simpson. Although the former Heisman Trophy winner from the University of Southern California was coming off a season in which he led the NFL in rushing with 1,251 yards, Saban believed Simpson hadn't even begun to scratch the surface of his extraordinary football skills.

In the Bills' season-opening 31–13 rout of New England, the Juice established an NFL single-game rushing mark of 250 yards, prompting Patriots linebacker Edgar Chandler to quip: "O.J. had more yardage than Secretariat."

The race for the record was on. Simpson gained more than 100 yards in each of his next four games, and after a subpar 55-yard effort against the Miami Dolphins' famed No-Name Defense

DID YOU KNOW...

That the only teams to hold O.J. Simpson under 100 yards rushing during his historic 2,003-yard rushing season in 1973 were Miami (55 yards), New Orleans (79), and Cincinnati (99)?

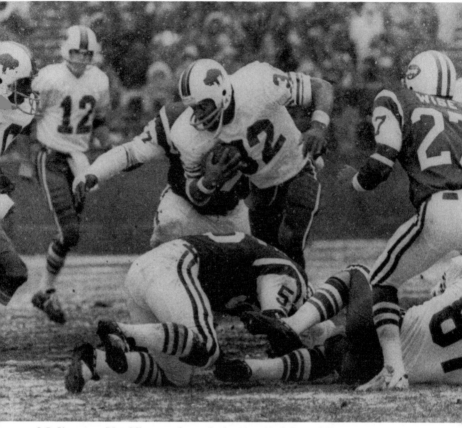

O.J. Simpson (No. 32) steps through the New York Jets' defense on December 16, 1973, at Shea Stadium in New York during the first quarter of the game in which he broke the NFL season rushing record.

in week six, O.J. rushed for 157 yards against Kansas City during a *Monday Night Football* game at Rich Stadium.

During that nationally televised contest, Howard Cosell called Simpson "the most powerful offensive force in football today." The national media began descending on Buffalo, and in every interview Simpson heaped praise on his blockers. Bills public relations director L. Budd Thalman also helped the linemen shed their anonymity by labeling them the "Electric Company," after a popular PBS cartoon show his kids used to watch.

"SURE, IF THEY BREAK BOTH HIS ANKLES."

—PATRIOTS COACH CHUCK FAIRBANKS WHEN ASKED IF THE NEW YORK JETS WOULD BE ABLE TO STOP SIMPSON FROM BREAKING THE NFL RUSHING RECORD IN THE FINAL GAME OF THE 1973 SEASON

"Any back who thinks he gets the yards on his own is a damn fool," Simpson said. "I wanted those guys to share in this because this was their quest, too."

The second half of the season started slowly for Simpson, but ended with a flourish. In the second-to-last game he made the Patriots look foolish again, gaining 219 yards on just 22 carries, putting him 60 yards shy of Brown's record and 197 yards shy of the 2,000 mark heading into the season finale against the Jets.

Simpson thought he had a shot at catching his boyhood idol in the record books, but he didn't think he would be able to go much farther on the snowy, slippery Shea turf. His teammates, though, sought to reassure him in the locker room before the game. "Climb right up my back if you have to," McKenzie told him.

During the Bills' second possession, Simpson carried for six yards, surpassing Brown. Referee Bob Frederic handed the ball to the running back, but McKenzie intervened, saying, "Juice is not done. We've got lots of work to do."

With about six minutes remaining, Simpson burst through the line for seven yards to go over 2,000. The game was stopped and his teammates carried him off the field.

After the game, he demanded that the Electric Company participate in his celebratory press conference.

In 1993, the Juice and his line mates were reunited back at Rich Stadium. Sadly, it would be the last time Simpson would hear

DID YOU KNOW...

That O.J. Simpson and Bubby Braxton are the top single-season rushing duo in Bills history? Simpson and Braxton combined for 2,640 yards in 1975—Simpson had 1,817 and Braxton had 823.

DID YOU KNOW...

That the 1973 Bills squad amassed a franchise-record 3,088 yards and 21 touchdowns on 605 rushing attempts? The Bills passed the ball just 213 times for 1,236 yards and four scores that season. With O.J. doing most of the toting and the Electric Company blocking, no Bills team has been able to grind it out like the 1973 club.

---

the cheers there. A year later, he was charged with and then acquitted of the double murder of his ex-wife and her friend in what many called the "Trial of the Century." Polls indicated that an overwhelming majority of Americans believed Simpson and his Johnnie Cochran–led "Dream Team" of attorneys had gotten away with murder.

"You'll never be able to hear O.J. Simpson's name or even watch the great vintage footage of O.J. Simpson as one of the very greatest players who ever lived without thinking of this tragedy," sportscaster Bob Costas said during an *ESPN SportsCentury* interview. "But that's the consequence of what happened."

FROM DISSING TO LOVING: JIM KELLY AND THE BUFFALO BILLS

As they prepared to affix his name to the Ralph Wilson Stadium Wall of Fame back on November 18, 2001, Jim Kelly couldn't help but think about what might have been. The flamboyant quarterback was going to be immortalized by the team and the city he had once spurned but came to love.

"It's funny how things turn out sometimes," said Kelly, owner of virtually every significant passing record in team history. "Looking back, I'm so happy Ralph Wilson didn't listen to me and trade me before I came to Buffalo, because who knows what would have happened."

To him.

And to the franchise.

Kelly campaigned hard not to come to Buffalo. After the Bills chose him in the first round of the National Football League draft in 1983, he bolted for the Houston Gamblers of the upstart United States Football League. When that league folded after just three seasons, Kelly continued to make disparaging remarks about the city of Buffalo and its pathetic football team, which was coming off a second consecutive 2–14 season.

"I'll never play there," he told reporters.

Kelly went so far as to threaten to sit out the entire 1986 season so he could become an NFL free agent. And he would have had the financial wherewithal to do it, because he had a personal services contract with former USFL franchise owner Donald Trump that would have paid him $800,000 had he not played.

"I was doing my best to make sure it wouldn't work out between me and the Bills," he said. "I wanted them to trade me to a team like the Oakland Raiders or the Pittsburgh Steelers. I wanted to go someplace where I would have a chance to win, and to be honest, I didn't think the Bills were committed to winning."

Several NFL teams, including the Raiders, contacted the Bills about acquiring the rights to Kelly.

"You had to listen because Jim seemed serious about not coming here," said Bill Polian, the Bills' general manager at the time. "I told [Wilson] about the offers, and he said no. Give Mr. Wilson credit. Refusing to trade the rights to Jim has to go down as one of the greatest decisions in franchise history."

Kelly had escaped once. Wilson wasn't about to allow him to get away again.

"HE'LL DRINK WITH THE BEST OF THE BOYS AND HE'LL SLUG IT OUT WITH THEM. HE DON'T CARE. WHEN HE THROWS AN INTERCEPTION, WHO'S THE FIRST GUY OUT THERE TRYING TO MAKE THE TACKLE? IT'S KELLY TRYING TO TAKE THEIR HEAD OFF. MOST QUARTERBACKS WOULD FALL FLAT ON THE GROUND OR RUN OFF THE FIELD. HE'S NOT LIKE THAT."

—FRED SMERLAS ON JIM KELLY'S TOUGHNESS

Despite not wanting to play for the Bills when he was first drafted, Jim Kelly fell in love with the organization and the city of Buffalo. He eventually set virtually every team passing record.

"I knew we were never going to turn things around if we didn't resolve the quarterback problem," he said. "Everything we had seen and heard about Kelly indicated that he was the talented and brash quarterback we needed."

The negotiations weren't easy. Rumor has it that the talks became so heated that at one point Polian was ready to drive-block one of Kelly's agents into the wall. Bills fans were so eager for a football messiah that they actually lighted candles in churches in hopes that divine intervention would convince Kelly to come to town.

Two weeks before the start of the 1986 season, the Bills made the quarterback an offer he couldn't refuse—the most lucrative contract in NFL history to that point, $8.5 million over five years.

With no other football options, Kelly reluctantly shuffled off to Buffalo and, to his surprise, wound up falling in love with the place.

His arrival in the Queen City created the kind of stir one might expect for the appearance of a pope or a president. A police motorcade escorted him, Wilson, and other dignitaries from the airport to a downtown news conference. As the procession cruised along the Kensington Expressway, the roadside was crowded with cheering fans.

Each of the city's network affiliates preempted national news for a live broadcast of the festivities. While photographers snapped thousands of pictures, Kelly fielded a congratulatory call from New York Governor Mario Cuomo. Once the star quarterback got off the phone, he quipped, "Maybe I'll take us to the Super Bowl and get a call from the president."

DID YOU KNOW...

That Jim Kelly almost died at age six when he went crashing through a glass door while chasing his brothers? Blood gushed from his jugular, and his mother pressed a towel to his neck to slow the bleeding. It took 40 stitches to close the gash and doctors told Alice Kelly that had she not acted so quickly, her son would have died.

Season ticket sales jumped by 10,000 within two weeks. A "KELLY IS GOD" banner was unfurled at the stadium then known as Rich for the quarterback's regular-season debut against the New York Jets.

"You have to understand that things had been pretty dismal for awhile," Wilson said. "What Jim gave us right off the bat was a sense of hope. Fans had reason to believe that better days were ahead. I'm happy to say that Jim lived up to his advance billing."

That he did. In 11 seasons with the Bills, Kelly established team records for touchdown passes, with 237; completions, with 2,874; and passing yards, with 35,467. He earned Pro Bowl honors four times and guided the team to an unprecedented four consecutive Super Bowls. And although the Bills lost all four of those championship games, Kelly eventually joined two other members of the great quarterback class of 1983—Dan Marino and John Elway—in the Pro Football Hall of Fame in Canton.

DID YOU KNOW...

That quarterback Jim Kelly caught two passes during his career for 40 yards, giving him an impressive 20-yard per reception average?

Success didn't come immediately for Kelly and the Bills. The team struggled to a 4–12 record his first season in Buffalo, and although the Bills improved to 7–8 in 1987, Kelly's finger-pointing rankled fans and teammates.

"Jim had a tough go of it at first, and I think he said some things out of frustration," recalled Kent Hull, the Bills' Pro Bowl center during their Super Bowl run. "I think through the years he

---

"I WOULD HAVE BEEN DEAD IF I HAD TAKEN SOME OF THOSE BLIND-SIDE HITS THAT JIM TOOK. I MEAN, THEY WOULD LITERALLY HAVE HAD TO SCRAPE ME OFF THE TURF AND CART ME TO THE FUNERAL HOME."

—STEVE TASKER ON JIM KELLY'S TOUGHNESS

Jim Kelly makes
an emotional
speech upon his
retirement from
the Bills following
the 1996 season.

matured. He earned the respect of every guy in that locker room
and the fans. People came to appreciate his toughness and his
leadership. They liked the fact that he was a linebacker who threw
the ball."

In time, the finest quarterback in Bills history came to realize
that Buffalo was the perfect match for him.

"I grew up near Pittsburgh [in East Brady, Pennsylvania]. And
Pittsburgh is an awful lot like Buffalo," he said. "You have hardworking people who love their football more than they do in
most cities, and who wouldn't want to play in a place where
people really care?

"With me, it never was about the city, it was about winning. I
didn't want to go to a place where I wasn't going to have the
people around me that I needed to win. When we were negotiat-
ing that contract, Ralph assured me that he was going to get me

---

"HE WAS ONE OF THE MOST UNSELFISH GREAT PLAYERS IN HISTORY. JIM TRULY DIDN'T CARE ABOUT HIS INDIVIDUAL STATS. HE CARED ABOUT HOW MANY WINS THE BUFFALO BILLS HAD INSTEAD OF HOW MANY TOUCHDOWN PASSES JIM KELLY HAD. HE MEASURED HIS SUCCESS BY THE TEAM'S SUCCESS, WHICH IS WHY, MORE OFTEN THAN NOT, HE WOULD AUDIBLE TO A RUN RATHER THAN A PASS. THAT TOLD YOU WHERE HIS FOCUS WAS. IT WAS ON THE TEAM."

—MARV LEVY BEFORE KELLY'S INDUCTION INTO THE PRO FOOTBALL HALL OF FAME

---

the supporting cast I needed. And I have to say that Ralph was true to his word."

Players such as Thurman Thomas, Shane Conlan, James Lofton, Will Wolford, and Steve Tasker were added to a roster that included Bruce Smith, Andre Reed, Darryl Talley, and Hull—providing Kelly with a team he could drive to eight playoff appearances and five conference championship games.

"I think people are appreciating that team all the more with each passing year," Kelly said in a 2006 interview. "We had not only great players, but a great coach in Marv Levy. We had a bunch of big egos on that team, and Marv made it all work."

But Levy said it wouldn't have worked without Kelly at the controls of Buffalo's fast-breaking, high-scoring, no-huddle offense.

"Jim had everything you wanted in a quarterback," Levy said. "He had a strong, accurate arm. He was tough as steel and a great leader. But the thing that stood out was his selflessness. He could have padded his passing stats, but it wasn't about individual stats with Jim. It was about winning. Looking back, that's what impresses me most about him."

Wilson appreciates what Kelly did for the franchise, too. There were some hard feelings between the two when Kelly entertained thoughts of coming out of retirement and playing for the Baltimore Ravens prior to the 1998 season, but things have been smoothed over.

"He was probably the most significant player in Bills history," Wilson said.

Kelly has kept busy in retirement. Though his Buffalo-based restaurant went belly-up and ESPN didn't retain his services as a studio analyst, he has remained in demand for card-show appearances and speaking engagements, and has even dabbled in auto-racing sponsorship. The biggest share of his time, though, has been devoted to raising funds for Hunter's Hope, a foundation he and his wife, Jill, established in honor of his late son, Hunter, who had Krabbe's Disease, a fatal neurological disorder that destroys the nervous system.

"We're a long way from finding a cure, but we are making progress," he said.

Jim was grateful that his son lived long enough to attend his induction into the Pro Football Hall of Fame on August 3, 2002. As a record Fawcett Stadium crowd of 17,700—including more than 1,000 of Kelly's friends and relatives—looked on, Jim paid homage to Hunter, who was seated in front of the stage in a wheelchair.

"Since the day I was elected to the hall [in early January of 2002], I prayed to God that my son would be here with me today," Kelly said. "God has granted me that blessing. It has been written throughout my career that toughness was my trademark. Well, the toughest person I've ever met in my life is my hero, my soldier, my son, Hunter."

Perhaps no one in the audience was beaming more that day than Jim's dad, Joe Kelly. The family patriarch had spent a lifetime scratching out a living as a machinist in western Pennsylvania. He didn't want any of his six sons to have to follow in his steel-toed bootsteps.

Joe's firstborn, Pat Kelly, went on to play linebacker in the NFL. But the most talented of the brood was Jim, and Joe worked him to the bone on the football field during the quarterback's

DID YOU KNOW...

That Jim Kelly remains the only quarterback in Bills history to toss 30 or more touchdown passes in a single season, setting the team mark with 33 in 1991?

formative football years. When Jim came home from elementary school for lunch, Joe would have the 10-year-old practice rollouts and dropbacks and throw spirals at a clothesline 20 yards away.

"Jimmy had a gift that none of the others had, and I didn't want him to waste it," Joe recalled.

Joe saw football as an escape from the hard life he had endured. He wanted Jim to wear a football helmet rather than a hard hat. "I believed it could be a way out for Jimmy and the others," he said. "I wanted them to have better lives."

Jim wound up earning All-State honors at East Brady High School, 60 miles north of Pittsburgh, and was recruited by every major football school in the country. There's a famous story about how legendary Penn State Coach Joe Paterno offered Jim a football scholarship—as a linebacker.

> ## "IF THEY EVER MAKE A MOVIE ABOUT THE LIFE OF JOHN WAYNE, JIM KELLY SHOULD PLAY THE PART."
>
> —MARV LEVY

Jim's older brother Pat advised him to turn down JoePa. "I had played in the NFL and I knew Jim had the stuff to eventually make a living as a quarterback," Pat recalled. "I said, 'Jim, stick to your guns. I got beaten up playing linebacker and you've got the skills to play quarterback, so go with a coach who will let you play that position. That's where you belong.'"

Lou Saban, the two-time Bills head coach, convinced Jim to attend the University of Miami. But after just one season as the Hurricanes' coach, Saban bolted for the head coaching job at West Point, and Kelly wondered if he should transfer.

"Jim was all set to go to Tennessee, but Pat had heard that Miami had hired Howard Schnellenberger, and he had played for Howard in Baltimore," Joe said. "He told Jim to stay put at Miami because Howard loves to pass the ball."

Jim followed his older brother's sage advice. He stayed at Miami and pumped life into a program that has since won four national championships and spawned several NFL quarterbacks. Although Kelly suffered a season-ending injury that dashed his

Heisman Trophy aspirations three games into his senior year, the Bills selected him in the first round of the 1983 draft.

Kelly said he cried—tears of sadness, not joy—when he heard the news. He was about to reluctantly sign a contract with the Bills

DID YOU KNOW...

That Lou Saban recruited Jim Kelly to play football at the University of Miami?

when USFL representatives reached him at Rich Stadium. A secretary put the call through literally minutes before Kelly was going to put pen to paper, and the deal with Buffalo fell through.

Kelly wound up signing with the Houston Gamblers and lit up the fledgling league, passing for 83 touchdowns and more than 9,000 yards in just two seasons.

"Those two years there actually benefited him because if he had gone to Buffalo out of college, he would have sat behind Joe Ferguson for two years," Joe said. "I think sitting would have set him back. Playing those two seasons made him a much more polished quarterback."

Kelly didn't begin to flourish in the NFL until the Bills surrounded him with better personnel and adopted the no-huddle offense, under the urging of offensive coordinator Ted Marchibroda. His best two seasons were 1990, when he had 24 touchdowns, nine interceptions, and a 101.2 passer rating; and 1991, with 33 touchdowns, 3,844 yards, and a 97.6 passer rating.

Although his postseason stats didn't match his regular-season numbers and he is the only quarterback in NFL history to go 0–4 in the Super Bowl, he still wound up being a football savior in Buffalo. He may not have won the big one, but he was a winner. His record as a starter was 101–59. Twenty-three times, he guided the Bills to victory after erasing fourth-quarter deficits.

In time, he came to love Buffalo and Buffalo came to love him.

DID YOU KNOW...

That Jim Kelly threw for four or more touchdowns in a single game 10 times during his career?

"I'm glad Ralph didn't trade the rights to me because this was the best place for me," Kelly said. "It turned out better than I expected."

THE HIT HEARD 'ROUND THE FOOTBALL WORLD

The Bills selected Tennessee quarterback Glenn Glass in the second round of the 1962 American Football League draft. In the 13th round, they picked another Volunteer, tight end Mike Stratton, in hopes he would help convince Glass to sign with Buffalo rather than an NFL team.

But things didn't go as planned. Glass snubbed Buffalo, and the Bills were "stuck" with a tight end they didn't know what to do with when they opened training camp at the Roycroft Inn in East Aurora, New York, that July.

At first, Stratton practiced with the tight ends. But with Canadian Football League import Ernie Warlick firmly ensconced as the starter, the rookie didn't get many reps. Bills coach Lou Saban then tried Stratton at defensive end, but it wasn't until a rash of injuries occurred at linebacker that Stratton finally found a home.

"I had wanted to be a tight end because that's what I had been in college," Stratton recalled. "But sometimes others know better than you do what's best for you."

It proved to be one of the Bills' best position switches, and Stratton wound up being named to the AFL's all-time team. The eight-time All-Star picked off 18 passes during his illustrious career, which was immortalized when his name was added to the Ralph Wilson Stadium Wall of Fame in 1994. But the play for which Stratton will forever be remembered is the tackle he made on San Diego Chargers running back Keith Lincoln in the 1964 AFL championship game. The hit heard 'round the football world changed the game's momentum, and the Bills stormed to their first title with a 20–7 victory at old War Memorial Stadium.

Despite struggling to the Western Division crown with an 8–5–1 record that season, the Chargers were favored to defend their AFL title. The oddsmakers' faith was rewarded early on as

Lincoln broke free on a 38-yard run on San Diego's first play from scrimmage. Three snaps later, quarterback Tobin Rote rifled a 26-yard touchdown pass to Dave Kocourek.

After Buffalo punted, the Chargers were on the march again. But on a second-and-10 from the San Diego 34, Stratton made the play that would turn around the game and make him a permanent part of Bills lore. Rote called a flare pass to Lincoln in the left flat.

"The split end would run a curl, 10 or 12 yards down the field, and the key would be on the linebacker in a man-to-man defense," Stratton recalled. "If the linebacker came up, Rote could hit the curl. If the linebacker went back to help against the curl, you dump it off to the back. It was a win-win for the offense.

"We knew, though, that it was coming. I recognized the pattern when it developed and I tried to help as best I could on the curl, then get back up in time to cover the back. I started racing like crazy to get to the back in the event that he threw the ball to him."

And that is what Rote did. But Stratton's timing proved impeccable. The instant the ball touched Lincoln's fingers, Stratton drove his right shoulder into the running back's chest. The ball bounced harmlessly away and Lincoln crashed to the ground in agony.

"It was one of those bang-bang plays," Stratton recalled. "If I had been a split second earlier, it would have been pass interference, and if I was a split second later, he probably would have been able to juke me in the open field."

The collision not only knocked the ball from Lincoln's hands; it also knocked the elusive running back out of the game with broken ribs.

"When I got up, I just figured Keith would get up, we'd go back to the huddle, and we'd start all over again on the next play,"

"AFTER THAT PLAY, I COULD SEE IT UNWIND. I COULD SEE THAT WE WERE GOING TO BECOME CHAMPIONS OF THE AMERICAN FOOTBALL LEAGUE."

—LOU SABAN ON LINEBACKER MIKE STRATTON'S FAMOUS HIT DURING THE 1964 TITLE GAME

Stratton said. "When he didn't go back to the huddle, truthfully, I was happy. I didn't want him to be hurt badly, but, good gosh, he'd already wreaked havoc on us before, and not to have him play certainly enhanced our chances of winning."

Even Chargers coach Sid Gillman marveled at the hit.

"That was one of the most beautiful tackles I have ever seen in my life," he said. "That is the name of the game."

The hit took the juice out of San Diego's high-powered offense. The Chargers managed just 153 yards the rest of the day as Rote and his backup, John Hadl, were intercepted three times—once by Stratton at the Bills' 18 at the end of the first half to kill a scoring drive.

"That tackle kind of put the emphasis on what we planned to do," Saban said. "We were a rough-and-tumble group. We were great tacklers, great defensive people, and we loved to play tough when things were tough.

"After that play, I could see that we were going to become champions of the American Football League and we were ready to take on all comers."

On the ensuing series, the Bills scored on a Pete Gogolak field goal, and took a 10–7 lead in the second quarter on a four-yard touchdown run by Wray Carlton. Gogolak converted again before the half, and then in the fourth quarter Kemp hit Glenn Bass with a 47-yard pass, setting up a one-yard quarterback sneak for the final score.

But the play that made that title possible—the play still revered all these years later—was Stratton's tackle on Lincoln.

"Not bad," Stratton joked, "for an old tight end."

BACK-TO-BACK LEAGUE TITLES

After each Chargers touchdown—and there were many during that high-scoring 1965 season—a man in the end zone at San Diego's Balboa Stadium would shoot off a cannon. By day's end, visiting players and coaches were usually nursing pounding headaches and feeling very much like, well, cannon fodder.

Balboa's triggerman expected to have another busy afternoon when the Buffalo Bills came to town for the AFL championship game the day after Christmas that year. To be on the safe side, he purchased extra gunpowder.

It seemed like a prudent move because the oddsmakers had established the Chargers as solid favorites. The Bills' 20–7 victory in the previous year's title game in Buffalo was regarded as a fluke. Most figured there was no way the Bills would again bottle up Coach Sid Gillman's high-voltage offense, which featured the likes of John Hadl, Lance Alworth, and Keith Lincoln.

But as Bills owner Ralph Wilson recalled with glee: "It's funny how things work out sometimes, isn't it?"

Funny, indeed. A smothering Bills defense, led by all-AFL performers Tom Sestak, Ron McDole, Mike Stratton, and Butch Byrd, wound up stifling the Chargers en route to a 23–0 victory.

"The thing I remember most is that poor cannon guy," Wilson said. "He was all revved up to shoot that thing off, and then his team doesn't score. After the game, when the stadium was nearly empty, he dragged that cannon in front of our empty bench and fired it. He was so frustrated I guess he had to let off some steam."

> **"I CAN DESCRIBE THIS TEAM BEST IN THE WORDS OF MY FAVORITE TRAINER, EDDIE ABRAMOSKI. IT'S GOT A HEART LIKE A BLOWTORCH."**
>
> —LOU SABAN, ABOUT THE 1965 CHAMPION BILLS

Wilson laughed lustily as he recalled the incident. The solo cannon shot provided an exclamation point to a glorious and somewhat improbable season.

"Our '64 team was healthier and had more overall talent, but the '65 season may have been more gratifying because we had to overcome so much more," recalled Jack Kemp, the Bills' quarterback.

Injuries took a heavy toll on the Buffalo offense, as Kemp lost his two favorite targets—Elbert "Golden Wheels" Dubenion and Glenn Bass—one month into the season. The Bills offense was

Quarterback Jack Kemp (No. 15) was the leader of the back-to-back champion-ship teams in 1964 and 1965, winning MVP honors in '65. Photo courtesy of Bettmann/Corbis.

also hampered by the loss of the enigmatic Calton "Cookie" Gilchrist, a talented but petulant running back who was traded to Denver before the start of the season.

"We weren't nearly as potent as we had been," said Kemp, whose leadership skills were recognized by the sportswriters who named him AFL MVP that season despite his less-than-stellar passing numbers—10 touchdown tosses and 18 interceptions. "But we realized that we didn't have to score a lot because we had a heck of a field-goal kicker and a fabulous defense."

The kicker was Pete Gogolak, whose soccer-style approach wound up revolutionizing the game. He finished the season with a then-record 28 field goals, and had a foot in victories against Oakland and Houston.

The defense was superb, especially in the championship game, when it didn't allow the Chargers to penetrate deeper than the Bills' 24-yard line. "We had All-Star players at nearly every position on defense," Wilson said of the unit that didn't allow a rushing touchdown for 17 consecutive games.

"And maybe the best of the bunch was Tom Sestak, one of our tackles. He was a dominating force, much like Bruce Smith became for us years later. And nobody was tougher. Heck, Sestak played a half one time with a broken leg. Imagine trying to do that!"

> **"YOU HAVE TO BE QUITE A MAN TO PLAY HALF OF A FOOTBALL GAME WITH A BROKEN LEG."**
>
> —RALPH WILSON ON DEFENSIVE TACKLE TOM SESTAK

Because they performed before there was a Super Bowl, the wonderful Bills championship teams of the mid-1960s never got an opportunity to prove themselves against Vince Lombardi's dynastic Green Bay Packers.

"I've thought about that through the years," Kemp said. "It would have been a great experience. I'm not saying we would have beaten them, but it would have been very interesting. I think we could have held our own."

That Balboa triggerman who was forced to endure the sounds of silence over 40 years ago would probably agree.

BEEBE'S HUSTLE PLAY

Nobody thought much of the play at the time—least of all the man who made it. Yeah, it was good hustle on Don Beebe's part when he sprinted 60 yards down the field in order to prevent hotdogging Dallas Cowboys defensive end Leon Lett from returning a fumble for a touchdown late in the fourth quarter. But it had no bearing on the outcome of Super Bowl XXVII. The game had long since been decided. It merely prevented the Cowboys from tacking another score onto their rout of the Bills.

"I'm thinking no big deal," said Beebe. "Instead of losing 59–17 we lost 52–17."

As he trotted to the sidelines after stripping the ball from Lett, Beebe angrily yanked off his helmet. He was disgusted with himself and his teammates for the way they had played. The fumble recovery by Lett was one of a Super Bowl–record nine turnovers by the Bills. Beebe couldn't wait to get out of the Rose Bowl and head for some exotic island where people didn't know a football from a coconut.

It wasn't until after the game, in the morgue-like Bills locker room, that Beebe began to realize his all-out hustle might not have been in vain.

"I was sitting in front of my locker and I'm upset that we lost," he recalled. "But then Bills owner Ralph Wilson walked by my locker, shook my hand, looked me square in the face and said, 'Son, you showed me a lot today. That meant a lot to me, that a guy like you can represent the Buffalo Bills like that. Thank you.'"

In the days, weeks, and months that followed, Beebe received a ton of mail from people echoing Wilson's sentiments. Parents and coaches wrote to tell Beebe how much they admired him for not giving up despite the daunting circumstances. Some wrote that they hoped their children grew up to be like him.

In his book, *More Than a Ring*, Beebe recalled an especially poignant letter from a grateful father.

"I've never been able to reach my son," the man wrote. "We've never had a great relationship. Then, I see this play where you don't give up. I show my son this play and say, 'This is how you act in sports and in life.' Our relationship changed because of it. You'll never understand how much your action meant to a lot of people. Thank you."

By the time Beebe finished reading the letter, tears were streaming down his cheeks.

The play was the shining moment of the Bills' four Super Bowl appearances, and came to symbolize the relentlessness of those great Buffalo teams.

The fumble occurred with about five minutes remaining. Bills quarterback Frank Reich dropped back to pass and was nailed by defensive end Jim Jeffcoat. The ball popped loose and bounced into the arms of Lett, who was off to the races. Beebe had been out on a pass pattern down the field, and the instant he saw Reich cough up the ball, he was in hot pursuit of Lett.

"I never doubted that I was going to catch him," Beebe said. "I was just going to jump on his back."

As it turned out, that wasn't necessary, because once he got inside the Bills' 10-yard line, the lumbering Lett began celebrating prematurely.

Despite a drubbing in Super Bowl XXVII at the hands of the Dallas Cowboys on January 31, 1993, Don Beebe forever etched himself in Bills'—and sports—lore as he hustled back to strip celebrating Cowboys defender Leon Lett of a recovered fumble near the goal line to prevent a touchdown.

"Unfortunately for him," recalled Beebe, "he put [the ball] out there in his right hand and that gave me the opportunity to slap it away."

The football wound up bouncing out of the end zone, giving the Bills possession at their own 20.

Beebe had a solid career as Buffalo's designated speed-burner, with 164 receptions for 2,537 yards and 18 touchdowns in six seasons. In a game against the Pittsburgh Steelers, the former third-round draft pick out of tiny Chadron State in Nebraska had the game of his life, catching four touchdown passes to tie a team record for the most scores by a receiver in a single game.

But nothing else Beebe did ever had the impact of his play on Lett.

Among the mail items he received was a putter with a head made out of flat river stone.

"There was an accompanying thank-you note in which the gift-giver explained how he won a Super Bowl pool as a result of Beebe's hustle play, and that the prize was so huge he was able to start his own golf-club company," recalled Bills special-teams star Steve Tasker. "That was pretty cool."

What wasn't so cool was all the hate mail Lett received. Much of it was from angry gamblers who lost a bundle because they had the number "9" on their Super Bowl boards and would have won had Lett scored.

"One guy wrote that if he had lost money because of me, he would have hunted me down and shot me," Lett recalled. "It's scary to think about people getting that involved in this stuff. Yes, I made a mistake, but this was only a game."

51-3

Before they took the field for the AFC Championship Game at Rich Stadium on January 20, 1991, Marv Levy serenaded the Bills with his rendition of "One More River to Cross."

"As a singer," one of the Bills later related, "Marv is one hell of a football coach."

DID YOU KNOW...

That five former Bills went on to become NFL head coaches? They are: Tom Flores (Oakland and Seattle), Kay Stephenson (Buffalo), Marty Schottenheimer (Cleveland, Kansas City, Washington, and San Diego), Sam Wyche (Cincinnati and Tampa Bay), and Jim Haslett (New Orleans).

Rockne never warbled his "Win One for the Gipper" speeches, but the symbolism of Levy's lyrics wasn't lost on his team. They knew that there was one more river to cross in order to reach their first Super Bowl, and it involved the Los Angeles Raiders. The Bills had needed a furious fourth-quarter comeback to beat them during the regular season, and after that game some of the Raiders groused about Buffalo being lucky.

Levy made sure to dig out those quotes and post them on the locker room bulletin board before the championship game rematch.

"Coming into that title game, I could sense we were supremely prepared to make a statement," recalled Bills special-teams star Steve Tasker. "Still, I never expected to make a statement quite as loud as the one we did."

The statement they made could best be described as deafening. In the most complete and dominating performance in the franchise's storied history, the Bills scored 41 first-half points on their way to a 51–3 annihilation of Al Davis's boys.

Emotions ran extremely high at the stadium that day. The start of the Persian Gulf War was just days away, and patriotic fervor spread through the stands. After the band from West Point finished playing the national anthem, the majority of the spectators in the crowd of 80,324 began waving tiny American flags and chanting "U-S-A! U-S-A! U-S-A!"

"The best banner of the day," Tasker said afterwards, "wasn't 'JUST LOSE BABY' or 'WHO CARES WHAT BO [Jackson] KNOWS,' but rather the stars and stripes."

James Lofton breezes into the end zone for a second-quarter touchdown during a blowout of the Los Angeles Raiders in the AFC Championship Game on January 20, 1991.

The Bills set the tone early, driving 75 yards in nine plays on their first possession to go up 7–0 on a 13-yard pass from Jim Kelly to James Lofton. Buffalo was so efficient running the no-huddle during that march that the Raiders had to call a timeout after several plays in order to regroup.

The Raiders answered with a field goal, but that would mark the last time they were in the game.

The Bills' next drive resulted in a 12-yard touchdown run by Thurman Thomas. And that was followed by a 27-yard touchdown return of an interception by Buffalo linebacker Darryl Talley to increase the lead to 21–3. Kenneth Davis scored on short touchdown runs on the Bills' next two possessions and the rout was on. The Raiders were so discombobulated they tried all sorts of defenses in hopes of finding a combination that might stop Buffalo. But none of them worked.

The Bills' domination was borne out in the stats. They intercepted the Raiders six times and racked up 502 yards in total offense. Jim Kelly's 73.9 completion percentage broke the AFC title game accuracy record, and the margin of victory (48 points) also established a new standard.

The thing is, it could have been even worse had Levy not called off the dogs in the second half. Near the end of the game, some fans held up huge letters spelling out the word "Tampa," the site of Super Bowl XXV.

Perhaps no Bill was happier than Talley, the veteran linebacker who had endured back-to-back 2–14 seasons and the accompanying wisecracks. He related one of the cruel jokes for reporters that went like this:

"Knock, knock."
"Who's there?"
"Owen."
"Owen who?"
"Oh-and-10."

DID YOU KNOW...

That Penn State quarterback Richie Lucas was the first player drafted by the Bills?

On this day, Talley and his teammates had the last laugh. They made the Silver and Black feel black and blue.

TALKIN' PROUD

Some believed Chuck Knox had lost his marbles. Either that, or Ralph Wilson must have offered him part ownership in the Bills in order to lure him away from a Los Angeles Rams team he had guided to five consecutive divisional titles.

How else to explain why Knox would agree to take over the coaching reins of a Bills team in 1978 that had won just five of its previous 28 games?

Though the money Wilson offered was indeed close to a king's ransom, there was more to the story. "I saw it as a great challenge, and I like challenges," Knox recalled. "I felt we could go in there and turn the program around. That opportunity to build from the bottom up really appealed to me."

And so, Knox shocked the football world and shuffled off to Buffalo.

Shortly after settling into his new job, Knox pulled another shocker by dealing over-the-hill superstar O.J. Simpson to San Francisco in exchange for five high draft picks spread out over three years. The Bills wound up using one of those picks on running back Joe Cribbs, who became the focal point of their offense in the early 1980s. With the input of scouting director Norm Pollom, Knox also oversaw the drafting of wide receiver Jerry Butler, nose tackle Fred Smerlas, and linebacker Jim Haslett. The coach filled in other holes with the acquisition of veterans such as wide receiver Frank Lewis, guard Conrad Dobler, and linebacker Phil Villapiano.

DID YOU KNOW...

That the Bills have had three unofficial fight songs in their history: "Talkin' Proud," "Shout!", and "Go Bills!"?

The rebuilding of the Bills didn't occur overnight. Buffalo went 5–11 in Knox's first season and 7–9 in 1979, but the foundation had been laid for one of the more exciting, albeit brief, eras in team history.

The Bills rang in the 1980s with a 17–7 victory against Miami at Rich Stadium. The win snapped an NFL-record 20-game series losing streak against the Dolphins and set off a goal post–razing celebration.

The Bills wound up going 11–5 and winning their first divisional title in 14 years. Cribbs won AFC Rookie of the Year honors and the Bermuda Triangle combination of Smerlas, Haslett, and Shane Nelson stopped ball carriers with regularity.

The Bills' surge couldn't have come at a better time for a community battling double-digit unemployment after the closing of Lackawanna Steel. In hopes of boosting civic pride, the Buffalo Chamber of Commerce launched a feel-good campaign featuring a jingle called "Talkin' Proud" that wound up being played each time the Bills scored. The season ended on a sour note as Buffalo lost a close game to San Diego, but the team's future looked bright.

DID YOU KNOW...

That the Bills yielded just four rushing touchdowns each season during their AFL championship years, and once went 17 games without allowing a runner in their end zone?

The Bills went 10–6 in 1981 and beat the Jets in New York before losing in the divisional round of the playoffs against Cincinnati. The Talkin' Proud era came crashing down in '82; Cribbs staged a long holdout, and the Bills went 4–5 and missed the playoffs in a strike-shortened campaign.

Knox left to take a job as head coach with the Seattle Seahawks, and the Bills began a decline that would bottom out in the mid-1980s with back-to-back 2–14 seasons.

THE BAD

ormer Bills linebacker Darryl Talley was playing golf with some friends not long ago when one of his putts veered just to the right of the cup.

"Wide right, Darryl," quipped one of the smart alecks in his foursome. "No good."

Talley cringed and shook his head.

Even on the links, even close to two decades removed from Super Bowl XXV, there is no escaping the most memorable and most painful moment in Buffalo sports history.

Wide right, of course, is where Scott Norwood's last-second 47-yard field-goal attempt traveled that fateful night of January 27, 1991, in Tampa, Florida.

Wide right is where the thoughts of Bills players and fans invariably drift each Super Bowl season.

"You're clicking the remote and that damn lowlight comes up, and you pray that one freaking time that kick will hook just a few feet to the left," said Jim Kelly, the quarterback of all four Bills Super Bowl teams. "But it never does. It's always wide right."

Then.

Now.

Forever.

Of course, it never should have come down to that play. Norwood, who had given the Bills a leg up on the competition numerous times, never should have been put in that position against the Giants, who hung on to win, 20–19.

"That was the most visible play of the game, but it was all those invisible plays that caused us to lose," said Talley, who lives in Atlanta and runs a business that makes security barricades. "Missed tackles. Missed blocks. Dropped passes. Overthrown balls. Blown coverages. People still want to pin it all on Scottie, and that's bull. We all made contributions to that loss. I know I made my share of mistakes, and I told Scottie that afterward."

Indeed, had the Bills defenders not allowed the Giants to run the ball down their throats, Buffalo might have won, perhaps handily. Led by the helmet-rattling runs of Ottis Anderson, who gained 102 yards on 21 carries, New York controlled the ball for two-thirds of the game, wearing down the Bills defense and keeping Buffalo's high-octane, no-huddle offense off the field for more than 40 minutes.

> **"WHEN IT MISSED, MY WHOLE BODY WAS KIND OF DEADENED BY IT. I JUST FELT SO EMPTY OUT THERE."**
>
> —SCOTT NORWOOD, AFTER HIS 47-YARD FIELD-GOAL ATTEMPT, WITH SUPER BOWL XXV ON THE LINE, SAILED WIDE RIGHT

It was a masterful strategy by Giants Coach Bill Parcells, whose team entered the game as touchdown underdogs, in part because star quarterback Phil Simms was injured.

"Not only were we outplayed, we were outcoached," recalled Ray Bentley, one of the Bills' starting linebackers on that team, who went on to become a network football broadcaster and an Arena Football League coach.

"I don't mean that in a derogatory way against Marv Levy and our staff, but rather as a compliment to Bill Parcells. There was only one way for them to beat us, and that was by keeping our offense on the sidelines. That's exactly what they did."

The Bills had entered that game on an incredible roll. With Kelly distributing the ball like Magic Johnson on the break to double-threat running back Thurman Thomas and wide receivers Andre Reed and James Lofton, Buffalo stampeded the Miami

Dolphins, 44–34, in the divisional playoff game, then smoked the Los Angeles Raiders, 51–3, for the AFC championship.

"I don't know if we ever clicked better offensively than we did in those two games," Kelly said. "Just about everything we tried worked. We were in a zone."

Bills fans were in a zone, too. Many could not believe that it was really happening, that their team, after so many years of frustration and ridicule, was actually going to pro football's ultimate game.

Adding to the emotions of the week was the Persian Gulf War. With Scud missiles raining down in the Middle East, there were fears that Iraqi president Saddam Hussein might use the Super Bowl as the stage for a terrorist attack. The concerns were so real that NFL Commissioner Paul Tagliabue consulted with then-president George H.W. Bush about the possibility of canceling the game. But Bush was emphatic that the Super Bowl be played as scheduled.

Security in and around Tampa Stadium was tighter than ever. An Apache attack helicopter hovered just above the light standards and no planes were allowed within a seven-mile radius. SWAT teams were stationed atop the press box. Fans and media attending the game were required to walk through a series of metal detectors.

Patriotic fervor was at a fever pitch at the stadium known as the Big Sombrero before kickoff that Sunday. Whitney Houston whipped the flag-waving crowd of 73,813 into a frenzy with a rousing rendition of the national anthem.

"Words can't describe the feelings we felt running through that tunnel out onto the field," Bentley said. "Other than watching my wife give birth five times, it was the most emotional and vivid experience of my life."

The game was played at a level of intensity Talley has never felt before or since.

"That game had a little bit of everything," he said. "You had snot-bubbling hitting. You had the

DID YOU KNOW...

That according to Steve Sabol of NFL Films, the video of Scott Norwood's miss in Super Bowl XXV is among the organization's 25 most requested clips?

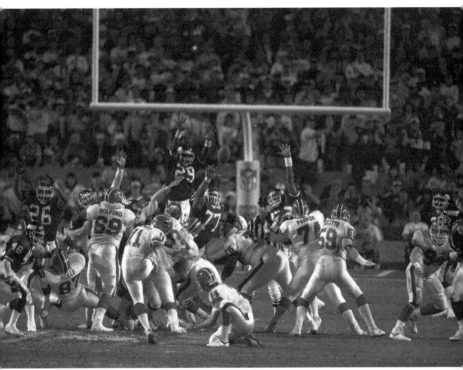

Scott Norwood misses wide right in his field-goal attempt on the Bills' last play of Super Bowl XXV, which clinched the game for the New York Giants, 20–19, on January 27, 1991.

fans going bananas, waving their flags throughout the game and chanting 'U-S-A! U-S-A! U-S-A!' and you had one of the most dramatic finishes of all time. Only a fool left that game early."

As Norwood lined up for the fateful kick with eight seconds remaining, Bills coaches and players held hands on the sidelines. Some closed their eyes and prayed.

Norwood hit the kick strong. Maybe too strong. The ball had plenty of distance, but not enough hook. It sailed a few feet wide of the right upright.

"When it missed," Norwood told a reporter, "my whole body was kind of deadened by it. I just felt so empty out there."

He could easily have hidden in the trainer's room afterward or taken the first cab out of town. Instead, he faced the music, answering reporters' questions for nearly an hour.

"IF HE WOULD HAVE MISSED THAT ONE, I WOULD HAVE DROPPED HIM FROM THE PLANE OVER MINNESOTA OR NORTH DAKOTA."

—THURMAN THOMAS TALKING ABOUT SCOTT NORWOOD FOLLOWING AN OVERTIME VICTORY VERSUS OAKLAND IN 1991 IN WHICH THE KICKER BOTCHED THREE FIELD GOALS AND AN EXTRA POINT IN REGULATION BEFORE CONNECTING ON THE GAME WINNER

"It was amazing the way Scott handled it," Bentley said. "I don't think I could have faced the press the way he did after something as personally devastating as that. I couldn't have been as gracious as he was reliving the pain. I don't think too many people would have been able to comport themselves the way he did."

Remarkably, the Bills shook off the shock of the loss and returned to the Super Bowl the following year. And the year after that. And the year after that.

They lost those games, too. But the feat of going four straight times may never be equaled.

"I credit Marv Levy for that," Kelly said. "He had a way of making you forget about past failures and look to the future. We had a resilient bunch of guys, and Marv knew what buttons to push."

Nearly two decades later, they seem to have come to grips with their Super Bowl futility. They look back with more pride than pain. And that includes Norwood, who did not, as some surmised, become depressed and suicidal in the years following the most crucial kick of his career.

"It's certainly something I can't change, be it positive or negative," said Norwood, who works as an investment executive in Centreville, Virginia. "I stand by the work that I did. It's a good career, an enjoyable career in the NFL. I didn't make them all, but I didn't miss them all, either."

There are still nimrods who vilify him for the kick that's become known as "the miss," and that irks many of his teammates, who are more than willing to share the blame.

"It's amazing that the one moment every kid dreams about—kicking that last field goal—happened to him, and then it went the wrong way," said Steve Tasker, the Bills' special-teams star who now works as a football color analyst with CBS. "People should realize your life goes on even if it does go the wrong way. I think he's put it in its proper place. But let's face it, it gets thrown up at him. He's like Bill Buckner."

And that's too bad, because, as Talley said, "Scottie had an excellent career. He missed a kick, but he made so many others that got us there. It wasn't fair to blame him. It still isn't, all these years later.

"The way I look at it and the way Scottie should look at it is that although things didn't turn out the way we wanted them to, we were involved in one of the greatest football games of all time. Wide right or no wide right, that was a game for the ages."

Bills owner Ralph Wilson concurred. "We never should have put Scott in that position in the first place," he said. "The thing people forget is that was a long, long kick. This was no gimme putt. This was a 30-footer with The Masters on the line."

To his credit, Norwood has remained a stand-up guy. That hasn't always been easy, particularly during the season after the miss, when the inquiries continued in torrents. Each kick prompted references to Super Bowl XXV. Jokes became cruel and pervasive. Talk-show callers began referring to him as Scott Nor*wide*.

"It was vicious at times," said former Bills special-teams coach

DID YOU KNOW...

That Scott Norwood had the most accurate field-goal-kicking season in team history in 1988, when he made 86 percent of his attempts (32 for 37)?

Bruce DeHaven. "I'd be in a restaurant and I'd hear people say things like, 'If Scott Norwood walked in here, I'd punch him in the face.' It's sad, but I don't think it represents the feelings of most Bills fans. The knowledgeable fans know that Scott won a bunch of games for us, and that he didn't lose that Super Bowl. We lost that Super Bowl. The whole team."

Norwood was released after the following season, and never kicked in the NFL again. He distanced himself from football for several years, turning down Bills alumni reunion invitations and interview requests. That fueled speculation that he was deeply depressed, that he had disappeared from the face of the earth.

"I just needed to create some space because the association between me and that one kick became too strong, and that disturbed me," said Norwood, who converted 72 percent of his field goals during his seven-year Bills career. "It was as if that was the only kick I ever attempted in my entire career. People forget all the kicks I had made before and after. I just grew tired of answering the same questions. I wanted to move on with my life and I didn't think I could if I was constantly rehashing that Super Bowl."

In recent years, he has become more visible. His wife hails from suburban Buffalo, and he has done alumni events, card shows, and interviews.

The fan mail still trickles in. A lot of it is from people who want his autograph. But some of the letters are from people who just want to tell him what a class act he was, answering all those questions the way he did after the most devastating moment of his football career.

"You'd be surprised, but the vast majority of the responses I receive have been quite positive," he said. "People have been very, very good to me. Sure, I wish I had made that kick, but that doesn't mean I'm not proud of the career I had. You have to take the good with the bad, and keep things in perspective, and I believe I have."

'71 BILLS WERE ZEROES

The sub–standard bearer for the Bills franchise is the 1971 club. That team should have been known as the Counterfeit Bills.

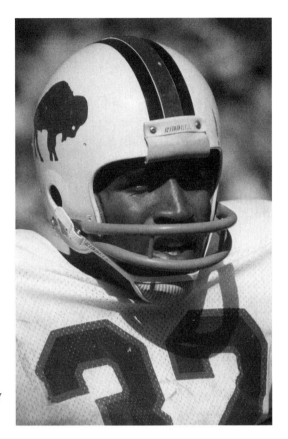

Despite having future Hall of Fame running back O.J. Simpson, the Bills were unexpectedly awful in 1971. Photo courtesy of Getty Images.

Coached by Harvey Johnson, the poor soul whom owner Ralph Wilson always called upon in a pinch, the '71ers opened the season with 10 straight losses on their way to a 1–13 finish.

Actually, that season had begun to unravel before it even started. Before training camp, longtime punter Paul Maguire retired to pursue a television career and former AFL All-Star defensive tackle Ron McDole was traded to the Washington Redskins. During a television interview that summer, Bills Coach John Rauch made disparaging remarks about the two former players. He said McDole was washed up and he called Maguire a clown who was more concerned with partying than football.

Wilson, who was fond of both players, was upset that Rauch went public with his criticism. At the start of training camp, he called in his coach and told him that he was going to publicly apologize to Maguire and McDole.

An incensed Rauch resigned on the spot and Wilson was forced to scramble to find a new coach ASAP. As he had done in 1968 after firing Joe Collier two games into the season, Wilson turned to Johnson, his pro personnel director, despite the fact that Johnson had led the Bills to a 1–10–1 mark in his first go-round.

"After John Rauch resigned, I'm walking over to practice at training camp and I see Harvey," Wilson recalled, chuckling at the memory. "I'm calling out, 'Harvey, Harvey, I need to see you.' And he knows what's going to happen, so he starts to walk in the opposite direction because he wants nothing to do with coaching again.

"Well, I finally track him down, and he reluctantly agrees to take over the job at the last minute. I felt badly for him because he'd much rather scout than coach, and we had an awfully inexperienced team that season. They were like a bunch of college All-Stars. I don't think Vince Lombardi could have done anything with that squad."

Imagine being asked to take the helm of the Titanic after it hit that iceberg, and you begin to appreciate the formidable challenge Johnson faced.

"Awful" might be too kind an adjective for the '71ers. Boasting future Hall of Fame running back O.J. Simpson and quarterback Dennis Shaw, named Rookie of the Year in 1970, the Bills were supposed to be a scoring machine. In fact, after dropping a 49–37 decision to the Dallas Cowboys in the season opener, Johnson said, "Nobody is going to stop us from scoring. Our problem now is to stop them."

DID YOU KNOW...

That old War Memorial Stadium, which was built in 1936 at the height of the Great Depression, was expanded over the years from 36,500 seats to 46,206 seats?

"YOU DIDN'T WANT TO GET TACKLED FACE-FIRST THERE ON A RAINY DAY BECAUSE THERE WAS A CHANCE YOU MIGHT DROWN."

—TOM RYCHLEC DESCRIBING THE PLAYING SURFACE AT OLD WAR MEMORIAL STADIUM

Talk about not knowing the score. The Bills proceeded to be shut out four times, averaging just 11 points the rest of the way.

How bad were those Bills? They were so bad that kicker John Leypoldt led them in scoring with a grand total of 39 points.

They were so bad that Shaw, who was supposed to be the next great NFL quarterback, finished with 11 touchdown passes and 26 interceptions.

They were so bad, their average score in defeat was 28–13.

Little wonder that late that season an embarrassed Wilson called his Bills "totally inept."

Simpson, who finished with a team-leading 742 yards rushing, said he was surprised the team didn't do a lot better.

"We thought," he told reporters after the last game, "that we'd do seven times as good."

To paraphrase O.J.'s defense lawyer, Johnnie Cochran, if the quote doesn't fit, the coach must quit. And that's what happened at season's end. Johnson went back to doing what he did best—scouting— and Lou Saban was hired as head coach.

> **DID YOU KNOW...**
>
> That in 1971, while the Bills were lobbying for a new stadium to replace the dilapidated Rockpile, there were reports the team might move to New York City and play in Yankee Stadium?

Saban's return for a second tour of duty with the Bills was a positive, as was the news that the Erie County legislature had approved $23 million for the construction of a new stadium in Orchard Park.

Replacing antiquated War Memorial Stadium, also known as "the Rockpile," had been a political football, and Wilson had seriously considered moving the franchise if something wasn't done.

There were even reports that the Bills might move to New York City to play in Yankee Stadium because the Giants were leaving for the New Jersey Meadowlands.

If current Bills fans are looking for some positive history to hang their hopes on, consider this: two years after the horrible autumn of '71, Buffalo reeled off consecutive 9–5 seasons and made the playoffs in 1974.

Even in those pre–salary cap jail days, you sometimes had to become very bad before you could become very good.

HOME RUN THROWBACK

The instant Steve Christie's field goal sailed through the uprights that January afternoon at Nashville's Adelphia Coliseum, the people in the visiting owner's box began acting as if they were at a hoedown at the Grand Ole Opry. And why not celebrate? After all, Christie's 41-yard boot had given the Bills a 16–15 lead over the Tennessee Titans. And with just 16 seconds remaining in that 2000 AFC wildcard game, Buffalo looked like a lock to advance to the next round of the playoffs, and perhaps even ride the momentum all the way to their fifth Super Bowl.

But Ralph Wilson wasn't ready to accept anyone's congratulations. More than 40 years as the owner of the Bills had taught him to wait until the final gun. He had learned to subscribe to the sage advice of former New York Yankees catcher and philosopher Yogi Berra, who warned, "It ain't over til it's over."

DID YOU KNOW...

That Gary McDermott wore No. 32 during O.J. Simpson's first training camp in 1969?

"I told the people in my box I wasn't ready to celebrate because there was time left on the clock and a kick to be covered," he said. "I'd seen too many strange things happen. I learned you can't celebrate until there is nothing but zeroes on that clock."

So, while others exchanged high-fives and hugs, Wilson kept his fingers crossed and watched nervously as Christie kicked off.

Tennessee Titans wide receiver Kevin Dyson returns a kickoff with seconds remaining in the fourth quarter to defeat the Bills 22–16 in their AFC wild-card game in January 2000. The ball was lateralled twice on the return and Dyson took it to the end zone.

What happened next was one of the most amazing and agonizing finishes in Buffalo sports history. The play, known as the "Music City Miracle," will forever rank down there with Scott Norwood's wide-right field-goal attempt in Super Bowl XXV and the "no goal" incident involving the Buffalo Sabres in the 1999

"MARV QUOTES HOMER; I QUOTE HOMER SIMPSON."

—WADE PHILLIPS, WHEN ASKED TO COMPARE HIMSELF WITH HIS BILLS COACHING PREDECESSOR, MARV LEVY

National Hockey League Stanley Cup Finals. It was another sad tale in which beleaguered Buffalonians couldn't help but feel as if they had gotten hosed by the Zebras.

Christie purposely looped a high, short kickoff that was caught by Tennessee's Lorenzo Neal, who immediately pitched the ball back to Frank Wycheck at the 25-yard line. With the Bills' cover men converging on him, Wycheck threw a lateral across the field to Kevin Dyson, who was stationed near the left sideline. Because several Bills defenders were fooled badly and did not stick to their coverage lanes, Dyson had a clear path down the field. With a convoy of Titans leading the way, he sprinted 75 yards for the go-ahead score.

"I was running down the field, and my heart sank because I knew I wasn't going to get there and there was no one else around and I knew he was gone," said Christie, who went from hero to afterthought.

The record crowd of 66,672 roared louder than a 747 revving its engines for takeoff as Dyson crossed the goal line. In Wilson's box, the celebration stopped instantly. Smiles were replaced by looks of shock and incredulity.

Bills coach Wade Phillips immediately called for a review of the play. He and his players contended that Wycheck's across-the-field toss to Dyson had been an illegal forward pass rather than a lateral.

Referee Phil Luckett agreed to give it a second look. For nearly three minutes, his head was stuck in the on-field replay booth, studying the throw from several camera angles. He concluded that the lateral was indeed legal, and announced on his stadium microphone that the play stood. The Titans' Super Bowl hopes remained alive. The devastated Bills were left to feel as if they had been jobbed again.

"Worst defeat in all my years in football," a dejected Wilson said afterward. "Worse than even the four Super Bowl losses."

Longtime football writers in the press box likened the bizarre finish to the Immaculate Reception play by former Pittsburgh

Steelers running back Franco Harris, who turned a pass deflection into a game-winning touchdown in a 1972 playoff game against Oakland.

Buffalonians, meanwhile, chalked it up to their ill-fated destiny.

"I don't know if it's the city of Buffalo or what, but it's a blue-collar, hardworking city," said Bills defensive end Phil Hansen, implying that western New York sports fans don't deserve this seemingly endless string of bad luck. "There was 'in the crease' last year with the Sabres and they get [cheated], and now this. It's just unbelievable."

Hansen, fighting back tears, didn't even mention Norwood's missed field goal or the three other Super Bowl defeats, but he didn't need to.

The Titans referred to the winning play as "Home Run Throwback." Tennessee special-teams coach Alan Lowry had filed it away after seeing Southern Methodist University use it to beat Texas Tech in the mid-1980s. The Titans had practiced it just once each Saturday that season—a total of 16 times.

DID YOU KNOW...

That Smith is the most popular surname in team history, with 13 players having worn that name on the backs of their Bills jerseys?

"We do work on it sometimes," said Titans linebacker Eddie Robinson. "But generally the feeling at practice is that it will never work."

The fact that Dyson wasn't even supposed to be on the field for the play made the result even more remarkable.

During practices, either Derrick Mason or Anthony Dorsett had taken the lateral. But during that fateful kickoff in the Bills game, Dyson was forced into action in place of both Mason, who was injured, and Dorsett, who was battling leg cramps.

"He [Titans head coach Jeff Fisher] just called my name out of the blue," Dyson said. "As we were running onto the field, they were trying to explain to me the gist of the play."

He definitely qualifies as a quick learner.

"I was real excited, especially considering how they tried to rub it in after they got that last field goal," Dyson said. "I saw No. 77 [Robert Hicks] over there dancing. I sprinted down past their sideline and waved bye-bye."

"HE'S NOT A PUNT RETURNER; HE'S A PUNT CATCHER."

—COACH WADE PHILLIPS ON THE ACQUISITION OF CHRIS WATSON FROM THE DENVER BRONCOS

Christie was the only Bill who had a shot at Dyson.

"I figured if I couldn't outrun a kicker, I didn't belong in the league," Dyson said. "If he had caught me I never would have heard the end of it."

The trickery wiped out a gritty performance by the underdog Bills, who had overcome their share of adversity before and during the game. In a controversial move the week before the wildcard matchup, Doug Flutie was replaced in the starting lineup by Rob Johnson. Despite the quarterback controversy that ensued, and despite the loss of two starters along the offensive line, the Bills battled the Titans hard, rallying from deficits of 12–0 and 15–13 to nearly win.

"One minute we've won the game, then it's gone," Christie said later. "I don't know what to say."

The Titans wound up advancing to the Super Bowl, where they lost an exciting contest to the St. Louis Rams. In an interesting twist, Dyson, the man who put the dagger through the Bills' collective heart, wound up being tackled a yard shy of the Rams' end zone with a chance to tie the game as time expired.

The last-second victory against Buffalo was a payback of sorts for Titans owner Bud Adams. Seven years earlier, his team, then known as the Houston Oilers, were victims of the greatest comeback in NFL history; Buffalo rallied from 32 points down to beat them in an AFC wildcard game.

"That was the greatest play in the history of football," Adams said after Dyson's last-second heroics.

Buffalonians in general, and Phillips in particular, would disagree with Adams. To this day, Phillips believes the play was illegal. He still refers to it as "Home Run Throw-*Forward*." Some crassly call it "Home Run Throw-Up."

Following the game, Hank Gola of the *New York Daily News* wrote: "If not for [referee] Phil Luckett's Immaculate Perception, another NFL playoff miracle would not have happened."

In Nashville, the play is known simply as the "Music City Miracle," and has achieved almost cult status.

Which shows that one city's miracle can be another city's nightmare.

"I thought it was legal," Dyson contended. "But when I saw the replay, it was a lot closer than I imagined."

Not surprisingly, the Bills saw it differently.

"This is the worst football feeling I've ever had," Buffalo defensive end Marcellus Wiley told reporters afterward. "And I'm sure I'm speaking for all my brothers in here."

It was Wilson's worst football feeling, too.

Even worse than those four Super Bowl losses.

SQUISHED BY THE FISH

Bills fans were happy to hear the American Football League was expanding in 1966. Their team was coming off back-to-back championships, and they figured the addition of the Miami Dolphins to the Eastern Conference would enable Buffalo to pad its record with two easy wins against the newcomers for several years to come.

The Fish, as they became known to Buffalonians, indeed proved to be easy prey that first season, as the Bills filleted them by scores of 58–24 and 29–0. But the 1967 season resulted in a split of the series, and by decade's end the Bills were only 4–3–1 against the new kids on the block.

DID YOU KNOW...

That nose tackle Jeff Wright snapped Dan Marino's streak of 759 pass attempts without being sacked?

And who could have guessed that after Buffalo defeated Miami 28–3 on November 16, 1969, at old War Memorial Stadium that more than 10 years would elapse before the Bills beat the Dolphins again?

Miami Dolphins safety Bob Petrella and his teammates dominated the Bills throughout the 1970s.

It still boggles the mind to think that the Bills went zero-for-the-decade against their South Florida rivals during the 1970s. You would have thought that just once the ball would have bounced their way against Don Shula's team, but it never did. Miami always found a way to win, and the Bills always found a way to lose during that stretch.

Buffalo's hatred for the boys from South Florida only intensified when Dolphins guard Bob Kuechenberg poured gasoline on the fire in 1974 by saying: "Buffalo will never beat Miami as long as I'm playing." It was a quote he boastfully reiterated in 1977.

It took awhile, but the Bills finally made him eat his words when they ended "the Streak" with a 17–7 victory on September 7, 1980, at Rich Stadium.

A crowd of 79,598 packed the joint that sunny day for the season opener, and when the final gun sounded, several thousand fans flooded the field and tore down the goal posts.

"It felt like we had won the Super Bowl," recalled Bills nose tackle Fred Smerlas. "That's how much people in Buffalo had come to hate the Dolphins."

Ralph Wilson was as ecstatic as the fans after the game.

"This is the biggest win in the history of the team...bigger than the AFL Championships," he told reporters. "I'll be happy to buy new goal posts."

> **DID YOU KNOW...**
>
> That Miami Dolphins great Dan Marino holds the record for most passing yardage against the Bills, with 7,553 yards, and touchdown tosses, with 50?

Although that win snapped Miami's streak against their AFC East brethren, it did not mark an end to the Dolphins' dominance. The Bills' futility against Miami continued as the Fish won 11 of the next 13 meetings in the series.

The tables did not turn until the latter part of the 1980s, when a team loaded with young stars such as Jim Kelly, Bruce Smith, and Andre Reed started getting the better of the club Buffalonians love to hate. During Marv Levy's tenure as Bills coach, his teams defeated Shula's Dolphins 17 of 22 times. One of those wins occurred at Joe Robbie Stadium during the 1987 season, when the Bills stormed back to win 34–31 on a Scott Norwood field goal in overtime.

"This was a turning-point win for this franchise," Buffalo general manager Bill Polian said in the ecstatic locker room afterward. "What are the odds of coming back after spotting Dan Marino a 21–0 lead?"

For the next decade, Bills-Dolphins would become one of the fiercest rivalries in football. Every game between the two teams seemed to have playoff implications, and players seemed only too happy to fan the flames. Sarcastic columns by Miami-area writers about Buffalo's

> **DID YOU KNOW...**
>
> That Ricky Williams of the Miami Dolphins holds the single-game rushing mark versus Buffalo, with 228 yards in a game on December 1, 2002, at Ralph Wilson Stadium?

"I WAS THE FAT KID IN THE NEIGHBORHOOD WHO WAS RIDICULED AND SUCKER-PUNCHED. I REALIZED EARLY ON THAT I WOULD HAVE TO FIGHT TO GET RESPECT. I THINK THE PEOPLE OF BUFFALO HAVE THE SAME MENTALITY. EVERYBODY WAS ALWAYS DUMPING ON THEM, ALWAYS SUCKER-PUNCHING THEM, SO THEY HAD TO FIGHT BACK. I THINK THAT'S OUR BOND. I CAN RELATE TO THEM, AND THEM TO ME."

—NOSE TACKLE FRED SMERLAS ON HIS RELATIONSHIP WITH BILLS FANS

---

cold climate and struggling economy enraged western New Yorkers, and Bills players fed off that.

"I hate Miami," Thomas spouted before a 1991 meeting between the teams.

The Dolphins provided Bills fans with some of their favorite villains. They despised the success Shula had against them in the 1970s and early '80s, and in their paranoid moments, accused the Don of NFL coaches of holding sway with the referees because he was a member of the league's rules committee. They feared and respected Dan Marino, the Dolphins' dangerous gunslinger quarterback. And they absolutely abhorred Miami linebacker Bryan Cox.

While coming out of the tunnel for pregame stretching before a 1993 game at Rich Stadium, the fans rode Cox unmercifully. He

---

DID YOU KNOW...

That on December 4, 1983, the Bills defeated Kansas City at Arrowhead Stadium, 14–9? They would not win another road game for roughly three years, and the victory that snapped their NFL-record 22-game road losing streak would also come at Arrowhead when they beat the Chiefs, 17–14. During that winless stretch, Buffalo lost games by an average score of 32–15.

---

claimed some shouted racial epithets at him, and he responded by showing them the middle finger of each hand.

Afterwards, Cox told reporters: "I don't like the Buffalo Bills as a team, I don't like them as people. I don't like the city, and I don't like the people. I wouldn't care if those people fell off the face of the earth."

Two years later, Cox was ejected from a Bills game at Rich after getting into a hockey-style fight with Buffalo fullback Carwell Gardner. It was not a pretty scene, and two Bills security men had to escort Cox off the field. The player began spitting and shouting obscenities at the fans, and some of them retaliated by swearing back at him and throwing full cans of beer.

The retirements of Kelly, Marino, Shula, and Levy in the late 1990s defused some of the rivalry's intensity. And since neither team has been especially good in recent years, the games don't matter as much in the standings the way they once did.

THE LOST DECADE

1970: Dolphins 33, Bills 14
Dolphins 45, Bills 7
1971: Dolphins 29, Bills 14
Dolphins 34, Bills 0
1972: Dolphins 24, Bills 23
Dolphins 30, Bills 16
1973: Dolphins 27, Bills 6
Dolphins 17, Bills 0
1974: Dolphins 24, Bills 16
Dolphins 35, Bills 28
1975: Dolphins 35, Bills 30
Dolphins 31, Bills 21
1976: Dolphins 30, Bills 21
Dolphins 45, Bills 27
1977: Dolphins 13, Bills 0
Dolphins 31, Bills 14
1978: Dolphins 31, Bills 24
Dolphins 25, Bills 24
1979: Dolphins 9, Bills 7
Dolphins 17, Bills 7

But that's not to say fans don't care a wee bit more when the Fish are in town.

"Just driving to the stadium on the bus, we see how much they hate us," said Dolphins veteran linebacker Zach Thomas, with a laugh. "The fans are throwing beer cans at the bus, mooning the bus, doing these other odd things.

"It motivates me, makes me think, 'Man, this is football.' It's a great place to play. I always look forward to going up there."

THE CASE OF THE MISSING HELMET

During speaking engagements, longtime Buffalo Bills equipment manager Dave Hojnowski follows his introduction with the line, "And I have no idea what happened to Thurman Thomas's helmet."

Before Super Bowl XXVI kicked off in Minneapolis on January 26, 1992, Thomas—the Bills' all-time leading rusher—lost his helmet and wound up missing the first two plays from scrimmage. The incident might have wound up being nothing more than a humorous footnote had the Bills defeated the Washington Redskins that day. Instead, it set the tone for a 37–24 defeat and became a part of Bills lore, not to mention Hojnowski's worst nightmare come true.

"Coach Levy is yelling at me and we're all scrambling to find it," he recalled. "We eventually found it at the end of the bench. At first, we thought somebody had stolen it. But I think what happened was that some player mistakenly thought it was his and picked it up, and then when he discovered it wasn't his, he just put it down. The problem is he didn't return it to where he found it."

Steve Tasker offered a different theory.

"Guys are superstitious, and I know Thurman followed a certain routine," the special-teams star wrote in his book, *Steve*

FODDER FOR LENO AND LETTERMAN

The Bills' Super Bowl futility gave standup comedians and sportswriters plenty of material for jokes. Some are quite cruel, and some have lost their luster because they've been repeated ad nauseam. Here are some of the more common Bills jokes.

- "B-I-L-L-S" stands for "Boy, I Love Losing Super Bowls."
- It takes four Ls to spell "Bills."
- What do you call a Buffalo Bill with a Super Bowl ring? A thief.
- How many Buffalo Bills does it take to win a Super Bowl? Nobody knows and we may never find out.

A helmet-less Thurman Thomas seemingly couldn't bear to watch his team lose to the Washington Redskins in Super Bowl XXVI on January 26, 1992—the infamous game in which he couldn't find his helmet at kickoff.

Tasker's Tales from the Buffalo Bills. "He would lay his helmet at the end of the bench before games. This usually isn't a problem because sideline security is tight most of the time. Nobody except players, coaches, equipment men, and trainers usually get anywhere near a team's bench.

"But Super Bowls are different. The pregame shows are huge and there are hundreds of performers, celebrities, and dignitaries who surround the bench. I think that Thurman put his helmet at the end of the bench and walked away for a moment. One of the assistant equipment guys may have picked it up because he was afraid someone might walk off with it. He probably put it under the bench for safekeeping, and then he got distracted while attending to one of the other players. When Thurman came over

> ## "KAY [STEPHENSON] IS GOING IN WITH A HANDICAP, LIKE A SWIMMER WITH HANDCUFFS."
>
> —FRED SMERLAS ON HOW PLAYER DISSATISFACTION WITH MANAGEMENT MIGHT AFFECT THE NEW BILLS COACH IN THE 1983 SEASON

to get his helmet after the coin toss, it wasn't there, and he frantically started searching for it. By the time he found it, he had missed two plays."

Thomas managed just 13 yards on 10 rushes that day, and was roundly criticized for not having his head (or his helmet) in the game. He had set himself up for some of the guff he took, because in the days leading up to the Super Bowl he had voiced his displeasure about not receiving enough credit for being the catalyst of the Bills' high-scoring no-huddle offense. His whining might have been taken seriously had he not been named the NFL's Most Valuable Player and had his picture splashed on the cover of *Sports Illustrated*'s Super Bowl edition that very same week.

Still, it's highly doubtful the Bills would have made a game of it even if he hadn't lost his helmet. The 'Skins simply were the better team, dominating Buffalo in every area.

PUBLIC ENEMIES

Throughout the years, there have been numerous players, coaches, commentators, and owners for whom Bills fans haven't cared. Here's a list of some of the men who have made them ill:

- Don Shula
- Bryan Cox
- Bill Parcells
- Mike Ditka
- Dan Dierdorf
- Bill Belichick
- Ben Coates
- Al Davis
- Howard Cosell

Not surprisingly, in the weeks, months, and years that followed, Thomas heard his share of jokes about his faux pas. And he didn't always handle the razzing well. At a charity softball game in Rochester, New York, a few summers after Super Bowl XXVI, he dumped water on a DJ who asked him where his helmet was as he walked to the plate. Thomas later threatened to punch a reporter who inquired about the dousing incident and also challenged a fan to a fight.

"He probably could have defused the situation by making light of it, but that wasn't Thurman's nature," Tasker said. "Things like that really ticked him off, and he used that anger as motivation."

Hojnowski, who has been with the Bills since 1977, used that embarrassing incident as motivation, too. Just to be safe, he and assistant equipment manager Randy Ribbeck now bring several extra helmets out to the bench during games.

"You have to be prepared not only for a misplaced helmet, but also for helmets that might crack during a game," Hojnowski said. "You try to be prepared for every possible scenario, but sometimes things happen because it's tough to keep track of 53 guys all at once."

> ## "YOU CAN'T MAKE THE MISTAKES WE MADE TODAY AND BEAT ANYBODY, EVEN LACKAWANNA HIGH SCHOOL."
>
> —QUARTERBACK JOE FERGUSON AFTER A 14–13 LOSS AGAINST THE BALTIMORE COLTS ON OCTOBER 21, 1979

SORRY SEASONS

Here are the worst teams in franchise history.

Year: 1971. Record: 1–13. Coach: Harvey Johnson. Gory details: The '71 Bills started with 10 consecutive losses. They were outscored by 210 points—an average of two touchdowns per game. The entire roster of quarterbacks combined for 12 scores and 32 interceptions during the season. Kicker John Leypoldt led the team with just 39 points. The only real bright spot was O.J.

DID YOU KNOW...

That the best defensive showing by the Bills occurred during a 37–7 thumping of Cleveland on December 12, 2004, when they limited the Browns to minus-three yards of total offense? The poorest showing by the Buffalo offense came during a 48–6 loss to the Oakland Raiders on September 15, 1968, when the Bills were credited with minus-19 yards.

UNLUCKY NO. 11

Never mind 13. Eleven might be the cursed number in Bills history. It was worn by Scott Norwood, who's been saddled with the albatross of "wide right"; Rob Johnson, whose career with the Bills will be remembered for a series of sacks, fumbles, and injuries; and Drew Bledsoe, who...well, see Johnson. Perhaps Roscoe Parrish, the current No. 11, might consider changing numbers. On a positive note, 11 is the number of consecutive wins the Bills recorded from December 8, 1963, through November 8, 1964—still a franchise record.

Simpson, who rushed for 742 yards. Before the season an optimistic Ralph Wilson had this to say about Harvey Johnson: "I don't envy him, but I think he can get the best out of our squad."

Year: 1968. Record: 1–12–1. Coaches: Joe Collier and Harvey Johnson. Gory details: Johnson was named the coach by owner Ralph Wilson after the team started the season with an 0–2 record. Their only win came against the Jets, when they intercepted Joe Namath five times. The Jets went on to win Super Bowl III. The Bills' quarterback, Jack Kemp, suffered a season-ending knee injury during the preseason. After that, the Bills went through five signal-callers, who combined for seven touchdowns and 28 picks. They lost their last eight games and were outscored by 168 points that season. The campaign's only bright spot was that the Bills' league-worst record enabled them to draft O.J. Simpson with the number one overall pick. Said Ralph Wilson at the end of the season: "I'm very embarrassed."

DID YOU KNOW...

That poor Harvey Johnson went 2–23–1 in two fill-in stints as the Bills' head coach? That's a pathetic .096 winning percentage.

Year: 1984. Record: 2–14. Coach: Kay Stephenson. Gory details: The Bills started the season with 11 consecutive losses.

They yielded a franchise-worst 454 points to their opponents—an average of 28 per game. Bills quarterbacks were sacked 60 times. Rookie running back Greg Bell provided some cheer in the midst of the team's misery, rushing for 1,100 yards. Said Fred Smerlas, reflecting on that forgettable season, "We were so bad, the only thing that showed up at Rich Stadium on Sundays were the snowflakes."

Year: 1985. Record: 2–14. Coaches: Kay Stephenson and Hank Bullough. Gory details: The Bills switched coaches after an 0–4 start. They were outscored by 181 points for the season. They

> ## "REMEMBER SAIGON IN 1975, WITH EVERYONE TRYING TO GET OUT?"
>
> —FRED SMERLAS, WHEN ASKED TO DESCRIBE WHAT IT WAS LIKE ON THE BILLS DURING BACK-TO-BACK 2–14 SEASONS IN THE MID-1980S

lost their last six games, including an 28–0 thumping by Miami in the season finale. Quarterback Vince Ferragamo, who was acquired in a trade for tight end Tony Hunter, threw five touchdown passes and 17 interceptions before giving way to some guy named Bruce Mathison. The team turned the ball over a franchise-record 52 times. At least Bullough's malapropisms—such as "We keep beating ourselves, but we are getting better at it"—kept fans smiling through their tears.

Year: 2001. Record: 3–13. Coach: Gregg Williams. Gory details: The 2001 Bills were outscored by 165 points for the season. They had a minus-17 takeaway-giveaway ratio, with just 19 takeaways, and committed a club-record 19 penalties in an early season game against the Colts. The quarterbacks were sacked

---

DID YOU KNOW...

That the Giants dominated the time of possession in Super Bowl XXV with 40 minutes, 33 seconds (versus 19 minutes, 27 seconds for the Bills)? The Giants' success came thanks to Bill Parcells's ball-control attack and the legs of Ottis Anderson, who gained 102 yards. Interestingly, the Bills still managed to average a point a minute—but they came up two points short.

DID YOU KNOW...

That during the 1984 and '85 seasons, when the Bills won just four of 32 games, they yielded a combined total of 106 touchdowns?

46 times. At least rookie cornerback Nate Clements kept things interesting, scoring on an interception and a punt return. Ralph Wilson started the season optimistically, saying, "If Rob [quarterback Rob Johnson] can learn to get rid of the ball in this new West Coast offense, I think he'll be a great quarterback." But Johnson lasted only nine games before suffering a season-ending injury.

Year: 1976. Record: 2–12. Coaches: Lou Saban and Jim Ringo. Gory details: The team started 2–2 but then lost their last 10 games, including a 58–20 decision to Baltimore in the season finale. Their opponents outscored them by 118 points during the season, and the Bills' defense was the second-worst in the NFL. Despite all this O.J. Simpson still managed to lead the NFL in yards gained, with 1,503.

THE UGLY

Marv Levy was involved in several compelling games during his long, Hall of Fame coaching career, but the Bills' 6–3 overtime victory against the New York Giants at Rich Stadium on October 18, 1987, wasn't one of them. To paraphrase Franklin Roosevelt—one of Levy's favorite historical figures—it was a game that will live in infamy.

"Yeah, I remember it," Levy says, smiling. "It was probably the worst game in pro football history."

Played at the tail end of the four-week NFL players' strike, the contest featured players who were literally Counterfeit Bills. Although it ended in dramatic fashion with Orchard Park, New York, native Todd Schlopy kicking the game-winning field goal from 27 yards, the game is better remembered for its ragged play. This exhibition of errors saw the teams combine for nine fumbles, five interceptions, five missed field goals, and 48 incomplete passes.

It was such a farce that Lawrence Taylor, the Giants' Hall of Fame linebacker who had crossed the picket line to play, occasionally lined up at tight end.

"I tried to convince [Giants coach] Bill Parcells to let me play running back and carry the ball a few times," L.T. recalled, "but he was afraid I might get hurt."

Or perhaps Parcells was afraid Taylor might hurt somebody.

One of the more humorous mismatches involved former Bills center Will Grant attempting to block the crazed linebacker. "Will got six holding penalties in the first half," Levy recalled. "I talked to him at halftime. I said, 'Will, you've got six holding penalties.' He said, 'Marv, for the amount of time I've been holding, that's good.'"

DID YOU KNOW...

That former Bills receiver Bo Roberson won a silver medal in the long jump at the 1960 Summer Olympics in Rome?

Levy did his best to keep his sense of humor during the strike, but deep down he worried that it might be his real team's undoing. He remembered coaching a playoff-caliber team in Kansas City during the first players' strike five seasons earlier. The work stoppage wound up tearing that team asunder and costing Marv his job.

The same thing had happened with the Bills in '82. They were coming off consecutive playoff appearances under Head Coach Chuck Knox, and with a potent offense—featuring the likes of gunslinging quarterback Joe Ferguson, dynamic running back Joe Cribbs, and the dangerous receiving duo of Jerry Butler and Frank Lewis—it appeared that Buffalo was ready to contend for a Super Bowl.

But after the Bills began the season with two victories, the strike struck, and the fans stopped Talkin' Proud. The 57-day work stoppage resulted in seven weeks' worth of games being canceled. When play resumed, it was obvious the Bills weren't the same team. They dropped their final three games to go 4–5 and miss the playoffs. Knox resigned a month after the season to take the head coaching job of the Seattle Seahawks. The Bills struggled to an 8–8 record in 1983, then plummeted to 2–14 marks and last-place finishes in each of the next two seasons.

"We had staged some practices on our own during that first strike," recalled Bills Pro Bowl nose tackle Fred Smerlas. "But they weren't very well organized, and before long, guys just went their own way. We just never had the esprit de corps when the season resumed."

To their credit, the real team stuck together during the 1987 strike. Their solidarity was evident during the two replacement games at Rich Stadium, as they picketed at the entrance of One Bills Drive. Under the leadership of Smerlas and veteran offensive tackle Joe Devlin, the team held regular workouts, and they appeared more ready to play than other teams when the strike ended.

Buffalo fans seemed to have little interest in the sham the NFL was passing off as real games. Only 9,860 spectators showed up to the 80,000-seat stadium on October 4 to watch the Counterfeit Bills play the Counterfeit Indianapolis Colts. The visitors wound up pounding the guys in the Buffalo uniforms, 47–6, as veteran NFL quarterback Gary Hogeboom tossed five touchdown passes.

That debacle was followed by a 14–7 loss in New England that saw the fake Bills turn the ball over five times. Mercifully, the strike was called off the following week, but not in time for the real Bills and real Giants to field real rosters.

Interestingly, the real Bills had treated the fake Bills acrimoniously through the first two games, but they began rooting for them in that Giants game because NFL Commissioner Paul Tagliabue refused to change his mind about the wins and losses counting in the standings.

> "I REMEMBER IT WELL. I'LL REMEMBER IT ALL MY LIFE. I THINK IT WAS THE WORST GAME EVER PLAYED IN THE NATIONAL FOOTBALL LEAGUE."
>
> —MARV LEVY, TALKING ABOUT THE BILLS 6–3 VICTORY AGAINST THE GIANTS DURING A 1987 STRIKE GAME INVOLVING REPLACEMENT PLAYERS

"It was awkward, rooting for scabs," Smerlas recalled. "But you really had no choice because they were going to have an impact on our playoff chances."

The Bills finished the season at 7–8 (one game had been canceled during the strike), and barely missed the playoffs. The motley crew, featuring NFL has-beens and NFL never-would-be's, contributed a win and two losses to that mark. Each of the players is listed in the team's all-time roster in the Bills' media guide. But there is a plus sign next to their names, indicating that they were replacement players.

THE BICKERING BILLS

Kent Hull was asked to put the Bills' tumultuous 1989 season into perspective.

"Look at it this way," the veteran center said in his Mississippi drawl. "We helped sell a lot of newspapers that year."

That they did. When it came to making news—especially the kind you expect to find in the rag sheets at the grocery store checkout counter—the '89 Bills were undisputed champions of the National Football League. Whether it was players ripping one another or coaches auditioning to become pro wrestlers, that season will go down as one of the most contentious in team history.

The genesis of the Bickering Bills can be traced to the fifth game of the season. Buffalo had come to Indianapolis with a 3–1 record and was in first place in the AFC East. But early in the game

Beleaguered quarterback Jim Kelly took and received his shots from teammates and the media during the forgettable 1989 season. Photo courtesy of Getty Images.

young offensive tackle Howard Ballard missed a block, giving Colts defensive end Jon Hand a clear path to Jim Kelly. Hand didn't merely sack the Bills quarterback; he separated his shoulder. Frank Reich replaced Kelly, but the Bills couldn't recover and wound up getting trounced, 37–14.

DID YOU KNOW...

That former Bills receiver Bobby Chandler once posed nude in *Playgirl* magazine?

The following day, doctors told Kelly he would be out at least three weeks. The quarterback was not pleased with the news and hung Ballard out to dry when he spoke to reporters. "I think four of the five positions [on the offensive line] are very solid," Kelly said, launching into his tirade. "I don't have to tell you guys what position they might have to make a change in."

The public lambasting of Ballard did not play well with the media, the fans, or Kelly's teammates. Three days later, the quarterback apologized for his remarks, but the damage had been done.

Two weeks later, following a 34–3 victory against the New York Jets, things became even more bizarre when Bills assistant coaches Nick Nicolau and Tom Bresnahan exchanged words and punches while watching videotapes of the game.

According to published reports, Nicolau, the team's feisty 5'9" receivers' coach, connected with an uppercut to Bresnahan's chin, knocking the offensive line coach to the floor and opening a cut that required several stitches. Nicolau then got Bresnahan, who stands 6'4" and weighs 260 pounds, into a headlock and rammed his head through a plaster wall in one of the offices in the Rich Stadium administration building.

During meetings with players later that day, Bresnahan wore a turban-like bandage around the top of his head and a Band-Aid on his chin.

The players initially thought Bresnahan had been in a car accident and had hit the windshield with his head. But when the receivers asked Nicolau what happened, he told the truth.

"Of course you can't hide something like that," said Steve Tasker, a special-teams standout and backup receiver for those

---

"JIM KELLY'S STILL THE QUARTERBACK, TED MARCHIBRODA'S STILL THE OFFENSIVE COORDINATOR, AND MARV LEVY'S STILL THE HEAD COACH. AND IF YOU DON'T LIKE IT, GET OUT OF TOWN."

—GENERAL MANAGER BILL POLIAN BLASTING REPORTERS AFTER A 22-19 LOSS
TO NEW ORLEANS DROPPED THE BILLS TO 8-6 LATE IN THE 1989 SEASON

Bills. "Once the media caught wind of it, it was like feeding time at the shark tank and we were holding the raw chicken. It just reinforced the public perception that we were a team in turmoil."

Nicolau and Bresnahan apologized to one another and went back to being friends. But the bickering among Bills players would continue.

During the taping of a local television show, Thurman Thomas was asked what position needed to be upgraded. Without hesitation, the Bills running back answered: "Quarterback."

A week later, appearing on a TV show with Paul Maguire, Thomas was asked about his caustic comment, and he stood by his remarks. Thomas told the viewing audience that Kelly wasn't perfect and should stop publicly criticizing his teammates. The you-know-what hit the fan as columnists and radio talk show hosts went to town on the pettiness that appeared to be tearing the team apart. In an attempt to put out the fire, the Bills held a news conference in which Kelly and Thomas read statements apologizing for their actions. They also told reporters that they would not be speaking to the media for the remainder of the season.

"It was very awkward, because it was staged, but I think it was something management needed Jim and Thurman to do in order to put this fire out once and for all," Tasker said. "I believe Thurman's stance really began to open up the lines of communication in our locker room. Guys actually started having honest conversations with one another, and the dialogue led to the friendships and the bonds that helped make us into champions.

"If Thurman had done that in a place like Miami, where Dan Marino was king, or San Diego with Dan Fouts at quarterback, I guarantee he would have been traded. Those quarterbacks would not have allowed any second-year guy to question their authority. But to Jim's credit, he didn't storm into Bill Polian's office and demand he jettison Thurman. Instead, he took what Thurman said to heart and realized his mistake."

Relations between team officials and the Buffalo media also became quite strained during the '89 season. After a late-season 22–19 loss to the New Orleans Saints at Rich Stadium dropped the Bills to 8–6, the occasionally combustible Polian went off on a few reporters in one of his more volcanic tirades.

"Jim Kelly's still the quarterback, Ted Marchibroda's still the offensive coordinator, and Marv Levy's still the head coach. And if you don't like it, get out of town," Polian shouted.

His comments only fanned the flames, and although he was attempting to take some of the heat off his coaches and players, it didn't work. The Bills fell to the 49ers in San Francisco the following week, meaning they would have to beat the Jets in New York in the season finale in order to make the playoffs. They wound up doing just that in convincing fashion, with a 37–0 pasting of their AFC East rivals. But expectations were not great heading into the postseason because they had limped home with three losses in their last four games.

The Bills traveled to Cleveland to play the Browns in the first round of the playoffs. They staged a furious comeback before losing 34–30. Kelly had a magnificent day, completing 28 of 54 passes for 405 yards and four touchdowns. His stats

DID YOU KNOW...

That Rich Stadium in Orchard Park was the first stadium to sell its naming rights? Rich Products Corporation, a Buffalo-based frozen foods company, held the rights for 25 years before the stadium was renamed for Bills owner Ralph Wilson.

might have been even gaudier had his receivers not dropped at least six passes.

The most infamous of those miscues occurred with the Bills driving for the potential winning score. Kelly lofted a perfect pass to a wide-open Ronnie Harmon in the back corner of the end zone, but the running back lost track of where he was and let the ball slip through his hands. On the next play, Browns linebacker Clay Matthews intercepted a pass to seal the deal. But something very important came out of that loss—the discovery that Kelly was a master at running the no-huddle. During that off-season, he lobbied hard to go to that offense full-time, and Marv Levy and offensive coordinator Ted Marchibroda decided to give it a try during the 1990 season. The rest, as they say, is history.

RUNNING OUT OF JUICE

He once was a source of great pride. But these days O.J. Simpson is a source of great embarrassment to Buffalonians—so much so that in 2006, Bills fans started a petition drive to have the former star running back's name removed from the Ralph Wilson Stadium Wall of Fame.

A town that once treated him like royalty now treats him as much of America does—as a social pariah who they wish would disappear to some deserted island, never to be heard from again.

Sadly, the man who forever will be remembered for being accused of murdering his ex-wife and her friend can't seem to stay out of the news. And each time he's back in the spotlight, Buffalo cringes more than most places, because he once was the city's favorite son.

"I WOULDN'T BUILD MY OFFENSE AROUND ONE BACK, NO MATTER HOW GOOD HE IS. IT'S TOO EASY FOR THE PROS TO SET UP DEFENSIVE KEYS. O.J. CAN BE A TERRIFIC PASS RECEIVER AND WE EXPECT HIM TO BLOCK, TOO."

—COACH JOHN RAUCH

Buffalonians were particularly saddened by O.J. Simpson's fall from grace. Here he celebrates his 1995 acquittal; however, he remains a social pariah, particularly among Bills fans, who had treated him like royalty.

What's happened to Simpson since those fateful events of June 12, 1994, still seems so surreal. Before he was accused of killing Nicole Brown Simpson and Ronald Goldman, the Juice had been one of America's most popular celebrities. And nowhere was his popularity greater than in Buffalo, the place where he had established numerous pro football rushing records as a running back for the Bills in the 1970s. His skills as a ground-gainer were electrifying and unparalleled. In 1973, Simpson became the first player in NFL history to rush for more than 2,000 yards in a season.

His good looks and infectious personality enabled him to transcend football. By the mid-1970s, he wasn't just running through tacklers—he was running through airports, doing

PASSING FANCY

O.J. Simpson completed only six of his 16 halfback option passes during his Bills career, but he made his connections count. Those six completions went for 110 yards and one score, and he was never picked off. That computes to an 82.8 career pass efficiency rating, higher than the career marks posted by full-time quarterbacks Joe Ferguson, Jack Kemp, Drew Bledsoe, and Doug Flutie.

national television commercials for Hertz. He eventually took his act to the silver screen. Although no one confused him with Laurence Olivier, he proved to be likable in movies such as the *Naked Gun* comedy trilogy.

Simpson later became a network football commentator, and further endeared himself to the citizens of his adopted hometown by unabashedly praising Buffalo on the airwaves every chance he got.

When he returned to Rich Stadium to report on the Bills during their Super Bowl run in the early 1990s, the affection between him and his legion of fans was readily evident. As Simpson made his way from the field to the broadcast booth, spectators would shout his name, ask for his autograph, and exchange high fives with him. He was more than just the most gifted athlete ever to wear their team's uniform. He was their spokesperson, their goodwill ambassador. He meant so much to Buffalonians because they always seemed to be battling an inferiority complex about their much-maligned city.

And that made the hurt all the more painful when Simpson was charged with double murder and became the lead actor in what would become known as the Trial of the Century. Although he was acquitted on October 3, 1995, he was found liable for the deaths of Brown and Goldman in a civil wrongful-death trial. In February 1997, Simpson was ordered to pay $33.5 million in compensatory and punitive damages.

Though he has not been asked back to Bills alumni functions since 1994, Simpson has returned to the Buffalo area on several occasions and has even attended games at Ralph Wilson Stadium. Some fans still sought his autograph during those games, but the majority of people ignored him as he watched from a corporate luxury suite.

In the fall of 2006, the Juice was making headlines again. Displaying a callous disregard for the Goldman family, Simpson signed a deal to publish a book called *If I Did It*, a hypothetical account about how he would have pulled off the murders. The book's publication was scheduled to coincide with a series of television interviews with Simpson. Fortunately, the public outcry was so great that the project was bagged.

> **"I'LL ALWAYS BE A BUFFALO BILL, AND I'M PROUD OF THAT. DO THEY CALL BABE RUTH A BOSTON BRAVE OR WILLIE MAYS A MET?"**
>
> —O.J. SIMPSON, AFTER BEING TRADED TO THE SAN FRANCISCO 49ERS IN MARCH 1978

Simpson's latest act of insensitivity infuriated Bills fans even further and energized the drive calling for the removal of his name from the stadium wall. If only it were that easy to erase him from their collective memories.

THE FLUTIE-JOHNSON SOAP OPERA

Though the main characters of this passion play are long gone, the mere mention of their names still evokes strong emotions among Bills fans. It's safe to say no issue in the team's 47-year history has ever been as divisive as the Doug Flutie–Rob Johnson quarterback controversy. One scribe wrote that it was "Bill Clinton and Monica Lewinsky in helmets," while former Bills defensive end Marcellus Wiley compared it to *The Young and the Restless*. Both analogies were on target; at the height of its lunacy, Flutie-Johnson was as juicy and as petty as a presidential scandal or a soap opera.

On one side of the great Bills divide you had Flutie, the diminutive Hail Mary quarterback who always seemed to find a way to answer a team's prayers. And on the other side, you had Johnson, a gifted athlete who was as fragile as a china doll and who could never seem to shake his Southern California surfer-dude reputation.

From 1998 to 2000, they were teammates battling for the starting quarterback job and the affections of Bills fans, players, and coaches. They did not coexist peacefully.

The genesis of this tempestuous relationship can actually be traced to the early months of 1998. Todd Collins had proven himself to be the "err" apparent to Hall of Famer Jim Kelly, so the Bills found themselves in the market for another quarterback. Confronted with a weak crop of free-agent NFL signal-callers, Bills general manager John Butler and pro personnel director A.J. Smith decided to travel the unconventional route and lure Flutie from the Canadian Football League. The 1984 Heisman Trophy winner from Boston College had bombed in his first NFL go-round with the Chicago Bears and the New England Patriots, but struck gold in the CFL, where the wider fields enabled him to take advantage of his superior mobility. Flutie wound up dominating north of the border, winning six Most Valuable Player awards while leading teams to four Grey Cups in eight years.

DID YOU KNOW...

That late film critic Gene Siskel of Siskel and Ebert fame once had Marv Levy as a summer camp counselor?

"I knew his contract would expire [at the end of the 1997 season] so that's when I started tracking him," said Smith. "I think he's a winner and a football player. I don't care about his size. People say it's a detriment, but the way the league has changed, you need to have a mobile quarterback. I like his instincts for the game. He pulls the trigger quickly, and he's one of the greatest competitors I've ever seen in any league at any time."

Flutie was eager to return to the States so he could prove wrong the detractors who said a 5'10" quarterback was too short to win consistently in the NFL. On January 20, 1998, he signed a two-year, $550,000 contract with the Bills, fully believing he'd be given a chance to beat out Collins, Alex Van Pelt, and Jim Ballard for the starting job.

But Flutie's euphoria didn't last long. On February 13, Butler announced that Buffalo had traded first- and fourth-round draft picks to acquire quarterback Rob Johnson from the Jacksonville Jaguars. At the news conference that day, Coach Wade Phillips announced that Johnson would be the team's starter.

A fourth-round pick out of USC in 1995, Johnson had backed up Mark Brunell in Jacksonville, but his value had skyrocketed during the 1997 season after a stellar performance in which he passed for 294 yards in a spot-start victory against the Baltimore Ravens. At 6'4", 215 pounds, Johnson was the ideal size for an NFL quarterback. He possessed a laser-beam arm and was extremely mobile. It also didn't hurt that he was 11 years younger than Flutie. By agreeing to give him a five-year, $25-million contract that included a franchise-record $8.5-million signing bonus, the Bills made it clear they believed Johnson was their quarterback of the present—and the future.

The news clearly blindsided Flutie, who couldn't help but feel as if he had been betrayed. Despite his anger, he realized there wasn't anything he could do about the situation. At that first training camp, he and Johnson appeared to be cordial to one another. Flutie offered advice and worked hard to get himself ready just in case.

It didn't take long for him to get an opportunity—and set into motion a quarterback debate that would eventually rip the franchise apart. Buffalo's 1998 opener would prove to be an omen, a snapshot of Johnson's futility with the Bills. In San Diego, the Chargers sacked him five times and knocked him out of the game early in the third quarter. Flutie came in from the bullpen and threw two touchdown passes to Andre Reed. He also moved the Bills into position for the winning field goal, but the normally

DID YOU KNOW...

That defensive tackle Tom Sestak, guard Billy Shaw, and safety George Saimes were the Bills named to the AFL's all-time team?

Clearly, the diminutive Doug Flutie (left) and the injury-prone Rob Johnson did not see eye-to-eye during their heated quarterback controversy.

dependable Steve Christie missed a 39-yard attempt with three seconds left.

Johnson was back in action the next week and struggled once more. The Bills lost to Miami and St. Louis before the young quarterback pulled himself together, playing magnificently in a 26–21 victory over San Francisco. Though Buffalo was 1–3 through four games, many believed better days were just around the corner; the game against the 49ers was a preview of what Johnson was capable of doing.

But, as would be the case throughout Rob's career, the injury bugaboo struck again in week five in Indianapolis. On the third play of the game, the Colts sacked Johnson and he fell awkwardly on the point of the ball, tearing cartilage in his ribcage.

Flutie would get yet another shot, and this time he literally stole the starting job from the fragile Johnson. The Little Quarterback That Could completed 23 of 28 passes for 213 yards and two touchdowns in relief, sparking Buffalo to a victory against the Colts. The following week, Flutie scored on an improvised bootleg with 13 seconds remaining as the Bills upset unbeaten Jacksonville at Rich Stadium. He wound up guiding Buffalo to the playoffs, and although the run would end with a close loss in the wildcard game in Miami against the Dolphins, Flutie had clearly established himself as *the* man in Buffalo. At age 38, he earned his first Pro Bowl invitation and was named NFL Comeback Player of the Year. His football renaissance led to the birth of "Flutie Flakes," which quickly became the best-selling cereal in western New York.

There was no quarterback controversy heading into the 1999 season. Flutie was solidly atop the depth chart. But his second season running the show would not be nearly as scintillating. His play declined noticeably, but the Bills still managed to win 10 of their first 15 starts. With Buffalo's playoff seeding already assured, Phillips decided to give Flutie a rest in the regular-season finale. In a meaningless game in which Indianapolis played many of its starters sparingly, Johnson went out and lit up the Colts.

Although the backup had played superbly, virtually everyone figured Flutie would start when the Bills met the Titans in Tennessee in the playoff opener the following week. But owner Ralph Wilson had been mesmerized by Johnson's play. This kind of performance was why he had shelled out $5 million per year for the young quarterback. Based on the Colts game, Wilson believed Johnson gave the team the best opportunity to go deep in the playoffs. Feeling pressure from his boss, Phillips dropped a bombshell at his news conference the next day, announcing that Johnson would start against the Titans.

> **DID YOU KNOW...**
>
> That Bills coach Hank Bullough once got trapped in an elevator at Rich Stadium before a game against Indianapolis?

"I think the team feels like we can win with either one of them," Phillips explained. "It's a tough decision, certainly, but it's something you look at objectively. I studied the film, it wasn't a haphazard thing. I talked to our coaches and I think it gives us the best opportunity to win this game. And I think our team has confidence in Rob. If they didn't, I wouldn't have made the change."

Though he said all the right things publicly, Flutie was furious over this breach of faith. He wasn't alone. Many of his teammates and at least half the citizens of Bills Nation thought Phillips was off his rocker. The news shocked the football world, and nowhere was the surprise greater than in the Bills' locker room. "You could have knocked me over with a feather when I heard that," said Robert Hicks, the Bills' 350-pound right tackle. "And that's saying a lot considering how big I am."

What had been a smoldering quarterback controversy had now become a raging fire.

Johnson struggled for much of the playoff game against the Titans' miserly defense, but staged a gritty comeback and guided the Bills to a 16–15 lead in the final minutes. But Buffalo's inability to defend against the Titans' trickery on the ensuing kickoff resulted in the Music City Miracle—and one of the most painful losses in Bills history.

DID YOU KNOW...

That Bills tight end Pete Metzelaars set an NCAA Division III basketball tournament record for field goal percentage while playing basketball for Wabash College in Indiana?

"That Tennessee thing was much more than a bloop kick and runback," said Christie, implying the quarterback controversy was what really did in the Bills. "Half the locker room was on one side and the others were on the other side. That's no way to go into the playoffs. You can't point blame one way or the other. It's just the players were confused. You need to be a solid unit, mentally and physically, going into the playoffs, and I don't think we were."

The divisions would only grow wider during the off-season. That winter, Flutie told a Canadian television station that the Bills would have won that playoff game had he started at quarterback. Johnson retaliated in a *Penthouse* interview when he said Flutie wasn't much fun to play with.

FLUTIE EARNED TOP RATING

If you were asked which Bills quarterback had the highest single-game passer rating, you'd probably guess Jim Kelly or Joe Ferguson or Jack Kemp. And you'd be wrong. Doug Flutie holds the mark with a 158.3 rating, in his final game as a Bill, in Seattle on December 23, 2000. Little Doug completed 20 of 25 passes for 366 yards and three touchdowns, and didn't throw a pick as Buffalo stampeded the Seahawks, 42–23.

Phillips declared an open quarterback competition heading into training camp. While that seemed like the fair thing to do, it wound up making the controversy even worse.

"The guys are divided because everyone likes Rob, he's a good guy and he's laid-back," Christie said. "But Doug gets them going much more when he's on the field. He changes things when he's out there. It's a different game with Doug."

Phillips's decision was made for him when Flutie suffered a groin injury early in camp. Johnson started in the opener—a prime-time rematch with the Titans in Orchard Park. But a sprained ankle knocked him out of the Tennessee game, and Van Pelt came in and guided the Bills to the winning field goal. Johnson bounced back to out-duel Brett Favre and the Green Bay Packers the following week, but struggled badly after that as the Bills lost three straight. He rebounded against San Diego, but was forced to leave the game with yet another injury, and Flutie engineered the winning points. With Johnson sidelined the next four games, Flutie seized the opportunity, playing well in a shoot-out loss to Minnesota before directing the Bills to victories against the Jets, Patriots, and Bears.

But the three-game win streak wasn't enough for him to keep the job, and Johnson was back under center for the Bills game at Kansas City.

Phillips's strange decision merely poured more gasoline onto the fire. In a *Sports Illustrated* article, an "unnamed player" was quoted as saying: "There's no question we're a different team with

Doug in there. All Doug thinks about is helping the team win and how he can do that. Rob seems distracted by things like wanting everyone to like him." Firmly convinced that Doug was the unnamed player, Johnson confronted Flutie. "I asked him about it and I was pretty ticked off," Johnson told reporters. Flutie denied it was him. The two didn't speak to one another the rest of the season.

Johnson did turn in one of his gutsiest performances in a 21–17 victory in Kansas City, scoring the winning touchdown on a 12-yard run. But what could have been another turning-point in his career was not. The Bills lost their next four games and fell out of the playoff race. Johnson was knocked out of action during the second-to-last regular-season game, and Flutie nearly manufactured a comeback win against New England. He started the season finale in Seattle, throwing for 366 yards and three touchdowns in a 42–33 victory against the Seahawks. It would be his last game in a Bills uniform.

DID YOU KNOW...

That before achieving fame as an actor—playing Superman on TV—Dean Cain unsuccessfully attempted to make the Bills as a defensive back?

A tumultuous off-season followed. The week of the Seattle game, general manager John Butler was axed. Not long after that, Phillips and most of his coaching staff were sent packing.

Tom Donahoe was hired as the new general manager and Gregg Williams was brought in to replace Phillips. The first order of business for the new Bills brain trust was the quarterback position. Interestingly, while working for ESPN.com during the 2000 season, Donahoe had written: "Flutie is 21–9 as the starter. What's the decision?"

But as general manager, he changed his mind. He and Williams said they had spent hundreds of hours reviewing film and interviewing people, including Flutie and Johnson, and had come to the conclusion that Johnson should be the quarterback. They also determined that there was no way the two could continue as teammates, so Flutie was cut loose.

"They hated each other," Williams acknowledged. "You like to have two quarterbacks who can both play, but you couldn't have that situation."

Johnson was relieved—to have won the job and to no longer have to deal with Flutie. "We just didn't see eye-to-eye from the first day," Johnson said. "I just think we're very different guys."

Flutie was angry that there was a perception that Johnson had beaten him out for the job. "If they truly believe Rob is the best guy for the job, then I have no problem with that," he said. "But shouldn't winning games count for something?"

Flutie would get one last measure of revenge later that year. One of Butler's first moves after becoming general manager of the San Diego Chargers was to sign Flutie. And later that season—in a game that Wilson strangely said was more important to him than the Super Bowl—Flutie scored on a late run to beat Johnson and the Bills.

Johnson's status as Buffalo's quarterback of the future didn't last long. In the eighth game of the 2001 season, he broke his clavicle against New England and was released after the campaign concluded.

On the second day of the 2002 NFL draft, the Bills traded a future first-round pick to acquire Drew Bledsoe from the Patriots. Though he didn't achieve the type of success the Bills were hoping for, Bledsoe spent three seasons with the team and provided some welcome relief from a quarterback controversy that had pitted Bills fans, players, and coaches against one another.

OTHER QUARTERBACK CONTROVERSIES OF NOTE

Long before Flutie-Johnson, there was Kemp-Lamonica. And although it was nowhere near as divisive as the mother of all Bills quarterback controversies, it did make life interesting.

The Bills, in one of their shrewdest personnel moves, had acquired Jack Kemp off waivers in 1962 from the San Diego Chargers, giving them their first legitimate quarterback. Kemp would go on to lead Buffalo to two AFL titles and throw for more yards than anyone in the league's 10-year history.

But his time in western New York wouldn't always be rosy.

In 1963, the Bills drafted Daryle Lamonica in the 24th round out of Notre Dame. Lamonica, known as the Mad Bomber for his ability to throw deep, became a fan favorite because of his strong arm and his Fighting Irish connections.

Like a baseball manager with a quick hook, Bills coach Lou Saban often grew impatient with his quarterbacks. So if Kemp was struggling, Saban wouldn't think twice about going to his bullpen.

"I've always believed that competition brings out the best in people, and I certainly felt that it helped both Jack and Daryle," Saban said. "I think if you look back on the results we had, it worked out pretty good."

That it did. Though Kemp started the lion's share of the games, Lamonica made some spot starts. And though the fans often serenaded Kemp with chants of "We Want Lamonica" when he was slumping, the competition between the two never created the divisions that the competition between Doug Flutie and Rob Johnson did.

While Kemp and Lamonica both wanted the number one job, their relationship never became frosty. "We were certainly rivals and competitors and I can't say that we were as close as we are today," Kemp said. "It wasn't mean-spirited, but it was certainly competitive—and I think competitiveness brings out the best in people. I could not understand why some fans could not accept the fact that every team needs not one but two quarterbacks."

DID YOU KNOW...

That former Bills quarterback Daryle Lamonica made his old team pay during an October 19, 1969, game by throwing six touchdown passes, the most ever against a Buffalo team?

Lamonica got his opportunity to be a full-time starter when he was traded to the Oakland Raiders in 1967 in what turned out to be one of the most lopsided deals in Bills history. He led the Raiders to the 1967 AFL championship game and a berth in Super Bowl II against the Green Bay Packers. He looks back fondly on his relationship with Kemp.

DID YOU KNOW...

That the coldest game in Bills history was against the Raiders on January 15, 1994? The temperature at kickoff was zero degrees, and the wind chill was recorded at minus-32. Buffalo took advantage of the frigid conditions to beat the Raiders, 29–23.

"I learned from Jack as his backup," he said. "Jack and I were always very close. He was my mentor."

Interestingly, there was one other quarterback controversy that never got off the ground, and it involved calls for Frank Reich to continue playing after Jim Kelly had healed from injuries. It was a debate that had little merit. Though Reich was a super sub, he wasn't a Hall of Fame–caliber quarterback like Kelly. And the two were best of friends. In fact, Kelly credits Reich "for being like a second quarterback coach."

ROGER AND OUT

Remember that gruesome broken leg Joe Theismann suffered while being tackled by Lawrence Taylor during that Monday night game in 1985? Well, Bills running back Roger Kochman suffered one every bit as horrific against the Houston Oilers on October 20, 1963.

The week before, Kochman had turned in a marvelous performance in Buffalo's 35–26 victory against the Kansas City Chiefs. The All-American running back from Penn State converted a Jack Kemp swing pass into a 63-yard touchdown run, and he also set up a Kemp touchdown sneak with a 48-yard sprint to the 1-yard line. With 86 yards rushing and 80 receiving, Kochman had established himself as an explosive, versatile offensive weapon who might be able to fill the void left by veteran running backs Wray Carlton and wide receiver Glenn Bass, each of whom had suffered season-ending injuries.

But the following week in Houston, Kochman's promising football career came to a painful end. While attempting to bull his way for a first down on a third-and-one, Kochman was crushed by two Oilers linemen—one of whom was 300-pound defensive tackle Dudley Meredith.

"The thing I think I remember most was lying on the ground, looking at the bottom of my foot," he said.

Longtime Bills trainer Eddie Abramoski and medics from the Oilers' staff attended to Kochman for several minutes before carting him off on a stretcher. "It was the most horrific injury I ever treated," said Abramoski, who served as the Bills' trainer for nearly four decades. "His skin was the only thing holding his foot onto his leg."

Kochman was whisked to Houston's Methodist Hospital, where he underwent emergency surgery for severed ligaments and arteries.

"The fortunate thing—if there was anything fortunate about the whole experience—was that the game was in Houston," Kochman recalled. "I ended up going to Methodist Hospital and was attended to not only by some good orthopedic surgeons, but the arterial damage that I suffered was supervised by Dr. Michael DeBakey, the world-famous heart surgeon who just happened to be in the hospital that night. They did a lot of work to save my leg."

DID YOU KNOW...

That 11 of Buffalo's starters from Super Bowl XXV were also in the lineup for Super Bowl XXVIII?

Kochman wound up suffering major nerve and circulatory damage and eventually had to have half his foot amputated. It took him three years to walk without the aid of a control brace.

Following his long, rigorous rehab, he went back to school to earn his master's degree, and wound up becoming an executive with Bell Telephone of Pennsylvania.

Through the years, other Bills have suffered scary medical moments. Cornerback Derrick Burroughs experienced temporary paralysis after making a tackle, and it was discovered that he had a narrowing of the spinal cord which forced him to retire from football. Receiver Don Beebe suffered several hellacious hits and concussions. And assistant coach Jim Ringo suffered a severely broken leg when he was accidentally pinned against the bench after a runner couldn't stop his momentum while heading out of bounds.

But Kochman's injury was by far the most gruesome.

"I remember coming back to the sideline after we had placed him in the ambulance, and that's when it really started to hit me," Abramoski said. "I started getting real queasy thinking about it."

THE DOG ATE HIS PLAYBOOK

When starting quarterback Todd Collins was forced to leave a game against the New England Patriots on October 12, 1997, in trotted backup Billy Joe Hobert. The Bills were high on Hobert, as evidenced by their decision to part with a third-round draft pick in order to acquire the 26-year-old signal-caller from Oakland in the off-season. One Bills scout went so far as to describe Hobert as "a Jim Kelly clone."

As it turned out, Hobert wound up being a clown rather than a clone.

Despite starting five games in four seasons in the league, Hobert looked as shaky as an untested rookie after replacing Collins. Two of his first three passes were intercepted, paving the way for a 33–6 rout by the Patriots. His performance was so bad that he was replaced by third-stringer Alex Van Pelt in the fourth quarter.

But the putrid performance wasn't what earned Hobert a permanent spot in the Bills Hall of Shame. It was his candid comments the day after the game, followed by a profanity-laced phone call to a local radio talk show a day later, that sent Billy Joe packing.

Twenty-four hours after the defeat, Hobert told reporters: "Every week, I've taken pride in knowing the game plan as well as the starter. This weekend was a joke. I screwed up. This is the first week I can remember where I only looked at the passing plays one or two times. I'm probably going to get in trouble for this, but I just didn't study the playbook hard enough."

While his honesty was admirable, his decision to slack off was not.

Bills fans were incensed. *You're making $750,000 a year and you weren't prepared? You got to be kidding me.*

Venom was flowing the next day on local talk radio stations as angry callers ripped Hobert seven ways to Sunday. For some reason, the quarterback wound up listening to one of the shows and couldn't resist phoning in. Hobert let loose with an expletive-filled tirade on air, and the Bills now had a full-fledged public-relations disaster on their hands.

The fans weren't the only ones angry. Bills coaches and players couldn't believe that Hobert had taken such a cavalier approach to a job for which he was handsomely compensated.

That Wednesday, Levy made the only decision he could make, handing Hobert a pink slip. "I told him it's unacceptable not to prepare as a professional football player in the NFL," the coach told reporters. "He didn't prepare and it showed."

> # DID YOU KNOW...
>
> That Baseball Hall of Famer Ernie Banks is O.J. Simpson's cousin?

"My approach is that if I have to go around kicking players in the rear, we shouldn't have them here in the first place," Levy continued. "But every now and then, a player could use some education... So if a healthy message derives from this, fine."

The message wasn't lost on the ex-teammates Hobert had let down.

"It definitely was a wake-up call," said tight end Lonnie Johnson. "It makes you prepare harder so you're not the next victim. I think the attitude now is that we need more preparation and a lot less laughing and joking."

Added guard Jerry Ostroski: "It's a privilege to play in this league. Everyone should have enough pride to prepare properly in order to play the best they can."

Hobert had been somewhat of a flake from the moment he showed up at mini-camp, so his faux pas didn't take everyone by surprise. A highly regarded quarterback who had taken the University of Washington to the national championship in 1991, Hobert could often be seen practicing his golf swing on the sideline during games.

He called his failure to prepare for the Patriots game one of the three most embarrassing moments of his life. He mentioned how, when he was a kid, a friend once pulled down his pants in public. As Hobert was about to tell reporters humiliating moment number three, a Bills public-relations man wisely whisked the quarterback away, saving himself and the team further embarrassment.

An interesting footnote to the Hobert fiasco: he was signed by the New Orleans Saints later that season and guided them to victory when pressed into action as an emergency starter. After the game, he admitted to reporters that he had indeed studied the playbook this time.

52–17

If beauty is in the eye of the beholder, then so is ugliness. And when it comes to ugliness in the Super Bowl, you'd be hard-pressed to find anything worse than the Bills' atrocious showing in Super Bowl XXVII.

The only thing more obscene than Buffalo's nine turnovers during their humiliating 52–17 loss to Dallas was Michael Jackson's pregame performance. The Thriller Man set a record for most crotch-grabbing during a Super Bowl.

The Bills' performance was also X-rated. They were actually still in the game with 3:24 remaining in the first half, trailing just 14–10.

DID YOU KNOW...

That Ralph Wilson owned stock in the Detroit Lions before forming the Bills?

But quicker than you could say Troy Aikman to Michael Irvin, they were down 28–10. Thanks to Bills turnovers on back-to-back possessions, the Cowboys' talented passing combination connected on two touchdown passes before intermission, and Buffalo never recovered.

Jim Kelly and Frank Reich threw two interceptions apiece and the Bills had eight fumbles, five of which they lost. The Cowboys scored five touchdowns off turnovers. You do the math. Five times seven equals 35—the margin of victory in Super Bowl XXVII.

A SNOW JOB

On a day when Minnesota Vikings quarterback Fran Tarkenton surpassed Johnny Unitas as the NFL's all-time touchdown pass leader, it was a throw from the stands that dominated the news. In the latter stages of a 35–13 loss at Rich Stadium on December 20, 1975, several unruly Bills fans began peppering the Vikings sideline with snowballs. One of the snowballs struck running back Chuck Foreman in the eye, causing his vision to blur and making him doubtful for Minnesota's playoff game the following week.

"The snowball barrage was the most ridiculous thing I've seen in 19 years of football," an incensed Tarkenton said after the game, undoubtedly forgetting the times when he and his Giants teammates were greeted similarly by disgruntled fans during games at Yankee Stadium. "The people of Buffalo ought not to be proud of what happened here today."

Interestingly, 24 years later the Bills drafted Foreman's son, Jay, in the fifth round. The linebacker from Nebraska spent three seasons with the Bills.

Through the years, Bills security men have had their hands full dealing with liquored-up, misbehaving fans. Once, during a *Monday Night Football* game, an inebriated spectator tried to cross a guide wire that held up a kicking screen behind one of the goal

DID YOU KNOW...

That the Bills actually did win a Super Bowl? It occurred during a 2002 made-for-TV movie titled *Second String*. Jon Voight played the Bills' coach, and there were cameos by former Buffalo quarterback Doug Flutie and play-by-play man Van Miller.

posts. Another time, fans doused ABC broadcaster Howard Cosell with confetti while he was taping his pregame intro with Don Meredith and Frank Gifford.

On at least three occasions, the fans have flooded the field and torn down the goal posts at Rich Stadium. Several spectators have climbed out of the stands during games and streaked across the field before being slammed to the turf by security guards in fluorescent windbreakers.

There were also scary moments at old War Memorial Stadium. During the 1962 season fans began flinging beer cans at Coach Lou Saban and his players when it became apparent the Bills were on their way to a fifth consecutive defeat.

"And most of the cans," quipped Saban years later, "were full."

IN THE CLUTCH

BILLS FANS GOT A KICK OUT OF STEVE CHRISTIE

Timing is everything, in kicking and in life. Bills fans—still haunted by the memory of Scott Norwood's miss in Super Bowl XXV—can't help but believe things would have been different had Steve Christie lined up for that 47-yarder.

Of all the kickers—and perhaps players, for that matter—in Bills history, no one was more dependable in the clutch than Christie, whom General Manager Bill Polian acquired as a Plan B free agent from Tampa Bay to replace Norwood following Super Bowl XXVI. It proved to be one of Polian's greatest personnel moves.

In eight seasons with the Bills, Christie connected on 78 percent of his field goals (234 of 299) and established team records for most field goals, extra points (309), and total points (1,011) in a career. In 1998, he set Bills standards for field goals (33) and points (140) in a season. Consistency was his hallmark. In 1994, he converted a team-record 17 consecutive field goals. It was one of four times during his career that he made at least 10 straight.

Clearly, no kicker in Bills history had a stronger leg. Christie booted the three longest field goals in Buffalo annals, with his 59-yarder against Miami on September 26, 1993, being the granddaddy of them all. He also set a Super Bowl record with a 54-yard field goal. His 70 percent success rate from beyond 40 yards for his career ranks him as one of the top five distance kickers in NFL history.

Christie made six three-pointers in an October 20, 1996, contest against the New York Jets in the Meadowlands—yet another club standard he owns. And it should be noted that he also had two other five-field-goal games.

Still, the thing that set Christie apart was his icy demeanor with the game on the line. That was never more evident than during the 2000 season, when in three different games he drilled winning field goals as time expired, tying a National Football League record for most walk-off three-pointers in a season.

"In terms of a pressure kicker, he's got to be as good as there ever has been," said Bruce DeHaven, the Bills' longtime special-teams coach. "The more the kick means, the better he is. He makes us all look good."

Christie's most memorable kick occurred in the famous 1992 wildcard playoff game against the Houston Oilers at Rich Stadium. His 32-yarder in overtime gave the Bills a 41–38 victory and capped the greatest comeback in NFL history.

"The guy is so reliable it's scary," Bills center Kent Hull told reporters after one of Christie's many game-deciding kicks. "I've never been around a field-goal kicker in my career where, once you get him to a certain point, it's automatic. That's the feeling we all have on this team."

The thing that makes Christie's resume even more impressive is that many of his pressure kicks were delivered in less than ideal conditions at Rich Stadium, where the gusts can occasionally turn a football into a beach ball and the turf can become as slick as ice.

DID YOU KNOW...

That the Bills drafted Heisman Trophy winner Ernie Davis with the AFL's first overall pick in 1962, but the Syracuse University All-American running back wound up signing for less money with the NFL's Cleveland Browns?

Steve Christie is lifted up by holder Chris Mohr after Christie kicked a go-ahead field goal with 20 seconds remaining in the fourth quarter of an AFC wild-card game against the Tennessee Titans in January 2000. The Titans then shockingly returned the ensuing kickoff for the game-winning touchdown via two laterals.

The weather, though, never seemed to bother Christie. That's understandable because he was used to the climate, having grown up in Oakville, Ontario, about 70 miles north of Buffalo. Soccer was his sport of choice as a boy, and he wound up playing for the Canadian Junior World Cup team. He didn't take up football until he attended the College of William & Mary, where he became both a kicker and a punter.

Undrafted out of college, Christie signed a free-agent contract with the Bucs in 1990 and promptly made the NFL's All-Rookie team that season. After the '91 season, Tampa Bay left him unprotected, and Polian pounced on him because he believed Christie's leg strength was perfectly suited to handle the difficult kicking conditions at Rich.

Some friends thought Christie was crazy for leaving a kicker's paradise like Tampa. But he had his reasons for heading back to snow country, and they had nothing to do with climate.

"You get depressed winning three games a year," Christie explained. "I wanted to go someplace where I would have a chance to kick in the postseason."

In Buffalo, he also discovered a place that would enable him to further pursue his favorite pastime—painting. From the time he was old enough to doodle with Crayolas, art had been a passion. So much so that he got as big a kick from putting brush to canvas as he did from putting foot to ball.

"Painting enables me to express myself in a much more creative fashion than football," said Christie, who majored in fine arts in college and now specializes in Abstract Expressionist oil paintings. "I'm fascinated by how you can create a mood through the use of different colors. I derive a lot of pleasure from it. It takes me away from where I am, gives me a chance to concentrate on something other than which way the wind is blowing and whether or not the field is wet and slippery."

There are similarities between his chosen disciplines. Kicking and painting are, for the most part, solitary endeavors. Each requires tunnel-vision concentration.

"The difference is that I can get up from the easel and get some coffee and come back to it in a few hours or a few days or a

---

DID YOU KNOW...

That special-teams star Steve Tasker holds the Bills' record for blocked punts, with six, while defensive ends Bruce Smith and Phil Hansen share the franchise mark for most blocked field goals, with four apiece?

---

few weeks and rework it," Christie said. "I obviously can't do that when I'm lining up for a field goal.

"Also, I don't have 80,000 sets of eyes focusing on me when I'm painting. Thank God for that. Can you imagine people cheering or booing each brush stroke? You'd never finish a painting."

One would think the many all-or-nothing propositions he encountered as a kicker would be nerve-racking. But Christie relished them. He said he was far more apprehensive several years ago, when he exhibited his artwork at a Buffalo-area gallery for the first time. Now *that* was pressure.

"Kicking a field goal in the wind and rain with everybody depending on you was a piece of cake compared to that gallery experience," he said. "I wrestled with my decision to put my work on public display.

"With football, there's an immediate resolution, immediate feedback. It's either good or no good. You're either a hero or a goat. It's different with art. Art is so subjective. Bruce DeHaven came to the exhibit, and he was saying, 'With art, you just never know how people are going to react to it.' And he's right."

Most of the people attending reacted favorably. Three of Christie's 16 paintings sold for roughly $1,000 apiece, and more would have been purchased had his wife, Alison, Steve's biggest fan, not red-tagged several of his best works.

"I just couldn't bear to part with them," said Alison, who festooned the walls of their houses in New York and Florida with Steve's work. "I see him in a lot of his paintings. The faces often are blackened out, but I can tell that it's Steve in the way the figure is folding his arms or standing. He doesn't notice it, but I can."

Not every person at the exhibit came away impressed. Some critics wrote that as an artist, Christie's a pretty good football player.

"The thing that bothered me was that they came with a pre-conceived notion that because I'm a football player, my stuff must be crap," he said. "I just wish they hadn't prejudged me, and had spent some time getting to know my work."

His football experience rarely influences his art. About the only time it did was with a painting he titled "Crossbars 1." It depicts a pair of metal poles, bent at crazy angles against a dark blue background. A cloth is draped loosely around the silver poles in the foreground. Christie said it wasn't necessarily what he saw each time he lined up for a field goal or extra point.

"It was just an abstract of what I had to look at every day," said Christie, who now works as a sports television commentator in Canada and helps out Camp Good Days and Special Times, a Rochester, New York–based organization that aids children and adults with cancer and other challenges.

"I sort of jazzed the painting up and messed with the pipes. I had originally planned to do a whole series of them, but I decided one was enough because I looked at crossbars every day at work. I didn't need to look at them all around my house."

While he hasn't yet shown anyone the Monet, he clearly was "money" with Bills games on the line. He was an accomplished artist on the football field. The only lament Bills fans have about Christie is that he showed up in Buffalo two Super Bowls too late.

AN UNLIKELY HERO

The Bills have been blessed with numerous clutch performers throughout their history.

Among them: the aforementioned Steve Christie; quarterback Jim Kelly, who guided Buffalo back from fourth-quarter deficits to victory 23 times; Frank Reich, the architect of the biggest comeback in NFL history, as well as some other lesser but still memorable comebacks; Doug Flutie, who proved he hadn't used up all his miracles in college; and Scott Norwood, who literally

PRESTON RIDLEHUBER'S STATS

- Two years in the NFL
- 22 games
- 12 carries for 55 yards
- Four receptions for 84 yards and two touchdowns
- One fumble recovery for a touchdown
- One pass completion for 45 yards and a touchdown

kicked the Bills to the AFC East title in 1988 with four game-winning field goals.

But of all the Bills players who stole victory from the jaws of defeat, none was a more improbable hero than Preston Ridlehuber.

A 6'2", 217-pound reserve running back from the University of Georgia, Ridlehuber spent just one season with the Bills. He was pressed into emergency action during a game against the Boston Patriots on October 11, 1969.

He seized the moment, rifling a 45-yard halfback option pass to receiver Haven Moses to give the Bills a 23–16 victory. The play would wind up being the highlight of the Bills' miserable 4–10 campaign, and it made the running back with the funny name a permanent part of Bills lore.

Ridlehuber wasn't totally unfamiliar with late-game heroics. The season before, while playing with Oakland, he had scored the clinching touchdown in one of the most famous games in football history—the "*Heidi* game," which saw the Raiders beat the Jets, 43–32. New York, which would go on to win Super Bowl III later that season, led that game, 32–29, with less than a minute to play. And even though Oakland was driving for a potential tying or winning score, NBC decided to pull the plug on the game at 7:00 PM on the East Coast so that the children's movie *Heidi* could be seen in its entirety.

As a result, much of the country missed a wild finish that saw Raiders quarterback Daryle Lamonica throw a go-ahead touchdown pass to Charlie Smith with 42 seconds remaining. On the ensuing kickoff, Ridlehuber recovered a fumble in the end zone for a touchdown, putting the finishing touches on Oakland's frenetic victory.

After the season, Ridlehuber was released by the Raiders and signed with the Bills as a third-string running back behind heralded rookie O.J. Simpson and backup Max Anderson.

Ridlehuber didn't figure to see much action that year because Simpson, the NFL's number one overall pick, was expected to carry most of the workload, with Anderson providing an occasional breather. But heading into their fifth game of the '69 campaign, Buffalo found itself without Simpson, who didn't dress because he had suffered a head injury the week before against Houston.

Anderson started in his place, but his shift was interrupted late in the fourth quarter when he was smashed in the face while being tackled near midfield by Boston's John Bramlett. The force of the blow was so great that two of Anderson's teeth were knocked out and six others were broken. He came to the sidelines a bloody mess, and Bills coach John Rauch sent Ridlehuber into the game.

Rookie quarterback James Harris, who had replaced an ineffective Jack Kemp earlier in the game, decided to try to catch the Patriots by surprise. He called for Ridlehuber to throw a halfback option pass. The play seemed quite risky because the running back had just come into the game and had to be rusty. Plus,

DID YOU KNOW...

That former Bills Coach Chuck Knox donated $1 million to endow a history chair at Juniata College in Huntingdon, Pennsylvania, his alma mater?

Ridlehuber hadn't gotten an opportunity to practice the play during the week because he was a third-stringer.

Ridlehuber took the handoff from Harris and began running to his left, then pulled up. The Patriots' defensive backs, thinking Ridlehuber was going to run, came up just enough to allow Moses to streak downfield behind them. Ridlehuber heaved the ball, and

Moses hauled in the surprisingly well-thrown pass for the game-winning touchdown.

"I would have rather had Harris run the play to the other side of the field," said Ridlehuber, a right-hander who had to throw back against his body. "I had to run to the left as I sought the receiver. I saw Haven downfield, but I didn't know if I could get the ball to him. I had a little trouble getting into throwing position, but I made it all right."

Ridlehuber also carried the ball four times for 25 yards as the Bills milked the clock on their next possession to ice the win. When Simpson returned to the lineup the following week, Ridlehuber went back to the bench, where he would remain for the rest of the season.

DID YOU KNOW...

That Bills defensive back Billy Atkins led the AFL in interceptions, with 10, and punting average, with 45 yards per boot, during the 1961 season?

An interesting side note to the Ridlehuber story: he was the first player in team history to wear No. 31—and that was by mistake. The number had never been issued before because it had been worn by the generic Bills player on the letterhead used by the club since its inception. For some reason, perhaps superstition, the equipment men had opted not to give it out, but someone wasn't paying attention the day of Ridlehuber's heroics. The following week, though, the error was corrected and Ridlehuber was given No. 36.

At the end of the year, the Bills released him and he never played pro ball again. Sixteen years later, when the Bills were on the brink of their second consecutive 2–14 season, a creative fan in the upper deck of Rich Stadium unfurled a banner that read: "WHERE HAVE YOU GONE, PRESTON RIDLEHUBER?"

That one pass back in the autumn of '69 was enough to ensure that Ridlehuber would never be forgotten by longtime Bills fans.

NUMBERS DON'T LIE
[OR DO THEY?]

everal hours after O.J. Simpson had become the first man in NFL history to crack the 2,000-yard rushing barrier on December 16, 1973, Bills public relations director L. Budd Thalman received a phone call. On the other end of the line was Seymour Siwoff, the head of Elias Sports Bureau, the league's official statisticians. Siwoff was calling to say that the stat crew at Shea Stadium had made a mistake when compiling Simpson's rushing stats in the Bills' regular-season finale against the Jets earlier that day.

Thalman's heart began pounding. Terrible thoughts stampeded through his head.

"I'm thinking the NFL's first 2,000-yard man is about to become the NFL's first 1,999-yard man," he recalled. "I'm thinking of all the people who are going to want to strangle me. Juice. Coach [Lou] Saban. Those big offensive linemen. I'm thinking about calling my real estate agent and the moving company so I can get out of town before this hits the papers."

Fortunately for Thalman, the mistake worked in O.J.'s favor. Siwoff said a review of the films showed that the stat men had shorted Simpson two yards, so his total would be increased to 2,003.

"I felt like a man on death row who had been granted a reprieve," Thalman said.

A VERY ORDINARY JOE

It's a good thing Joe Namath didn't have to face the Bills every week, or he never would have made it to Canton. Against Buffalo, he was "Way-Off-Broadway Joe." In 19 starts—nine wins, 10 losses—versus the Bills, Namath completed just 43 percent of his passes and had more interceptions, with 33, than touchdown passes (28). Buffalo had two five-pick games and one four-pick game against him.

His average per-game stat line against the Bills: 12 for 28, 191 yards, 1.47 touchdown passes, 1.74 interceptions.

Namath, of course, will always be remembered for his "guaranteed" victory in Super Bowl III. But two other games left an indelible mark on longtime Bills fans.

The first occurred during Buffalo's miserable 1968 season. In fact, it resulted in the Bills' only victory that year.

On September 29, 1968, at War Memorial Stadium, their secondary intercepted Joe Willie five times and returned three of them for touchdowns in a 37–35 win. Safety Tom Janik started the parade to the Jets' end zone early in the second quarter when he returned a Namath pass 100 yards. In a one-minute span early in the fourth quarter, cornerbacks Butch Byrd and Booker Edgerson got into the act. Byrd returned an interception 53 yards for a score and Edgerson followed suit with a 45-yard return for a touchdown, giving the Bills a commanding 16-point lead.

DID YOU KNOW...

That Elijah Pitts was the only African American to serve as Bills head coach, going 1–2 during the 1995 season while filling in for Marv Levy?

The Jets staged a furious comeback as Namath tossed touchdown passes of three yards to fullback Matt Snell and 10 yards to wide receiver George Sauer, but it was too little, too late.

"I didn't throw very well and they had great coverage," Namath said after completing just 19 of 43 passes for 280 yards and four scores. "Someone asked if we took the Bills lightly, that we weren't up for the game. Not true. We've never had an easy game in Buffalo.

Jets Hall of Famer Joe Namath (No. 12) rarely played his best against the Bills, particularly in the downpour of this game in which neither quarterback could throw the ball. Photo courtesy of Bettmann/Corbis.

What won it for them was their five interceptions—and that's my fault."

Bills Coach Harvey Johnson was understandably pleased with his team's effort, which included a record 235 yards in interception returns. After the game, he jokingly told owner Ralph Wilson that he was going to have to hit him up for a few drinks. "Maybe there won't be many more opportunities," Johnson said, not realizing how prophetic his words were. "So I'm going to get you now."

The other memorable Namath-Bills game had more to do with the crazy weather than with the Buffalo defense. It occurred at

Rich Stadium on September 29, 1974—a day that will live in infamy as far as Broadway Joe is concerned. With winds off Lake Erie gusting up to 40 miles per hour and rain coming down horizontally, neither Namath nor Bills quarterback Joe Ferguson could get anything going through the air. Namath finished with just two completions in 18 attempts for 33 yards and three interceptions, while Fergy failed to complete either of the two passes he attempted.

It was the only time in team history that the Bills didn't complete a pass, but on this blustery day they didn't need to. O.J. Simpson carried 31 times for 117 yards and Bubby Braxton had 17 carries for 84 yards. Buffalo won the wind fest, 16–12.

"If this were a golf tournament, they would have called it off," Namath said after the game. "But the conditions were the same for both teams and the Bills won. Sure, it was frustrating when you can't perform to the best of your abilities."

Wind or calm, he rarely could perform to the best of his abilities against the Bills.

WINNINGEST QUARTERBACKS

Here's a look at the top 10 starting quarterbacks in Bills history based on career wins through the 2006 season:

	Player	Wins–Losses	Percentage
1.	Jim Kelly	101–59	.631
2.	Joe Ferguson	78–84	.481
3.	Jack Kemp	40–29	.580
4.	Drew Bledsoe	23–25	.479
5.	Doug Flutie	22–13	.629
6.	Daryle Lamonica	10–4	.714
7.	J.P. Losman	8–16	.333
8.	Dennis Shaw	8–28	.222
9.	Todd Collins	7–9	.438
10.	Rob Johnson	7–15	.318

SUPER WOES

A comparison of the Bills and their opponents from Super Bowls XXV–XXVIII:

	Bills	Opponents
Points	73	139
Passing completions/ attempts/percentage	89/161, 55 percent	79/122, 65 percent
Passing yards	926	981
Rushing attempts/yards	99/404	143/571
Total plays/yards	260/1,330	265/1,552
Interceptions	2	9
Fumbles/lost	18/8	4/2
Sacks/yards	5/13	13/108

BOWLED OVER

You can cull many ugly stats from Buffalo's four Super Bowl defeats, but no number is more revealing or damning than their takeaway-giveaway ratio. The Bills were an incredible minus-13 in that department, which explains why they were 0–4 in the big game and were outscored by an average of 17 points.

Starting quarterback Jim Kelly and backup Frank Reich combined for nine interceptions and just three touchdown passes in

> "YOU THINK ABOUT WHAT MIGHT HAVE BEEN HAD WE WON NOT JUST ONE OF THOSE GAMES, BUT ALL FOUR. I'M GREEDY. I WANTED TO WIN THEM ALL, BUT GEE, IF IT WAS JUST ONE, HOW KIND WOULD HISTORY BE? WE HAVE A NUMBER OF GUYS WHO WILL GO TO CANTON AND A NUMBER OF US WILL BE SITTING ON THE FENCE, NOT KNOWING AND WONDERING."
>
> —DARRYL TALLEY, REFLECTING ON THE FOUR SUPER BOWL LOSSES

> ## "IT CAN NEVER GO AWAY. IT'S SOMETHING WE'LL LIVE WITH THE REST OF OUR LIVES. YOU ONLY GET SO MANY BITES AT THE APPLE. ULTIMATELY, THAT'S IT. WE DID EVERYTHING ELSE WE COULD."
>
> —DARRYL TALLEY ON THE BILLS' 0–4 SUPER BOWL RECORD

---

161 attempts, while their counterparts combined for seven scores and just two picks.

Fumbles were even more damaging. The Bills mishandled the ball 18 times and lost eight of them—three of which were returned for touchdowns. By contrast, their Super Bowl opponents fumbled four times, losing just two of them.

Buffalo also lost the sack-protection battle, yielding 13 for a loss of 108 yards, while only getting to the quarterback five times themselves for a harmless loss of 13 yards.

Opponents averaged 36 rushes for 143 yards. The Bills, because they fell behind badly in two of the contests, were forced to throw much more—which led to the high number of sacks, forced fumbles, and interceptions.

IT AIN'T OVER TIL IT'S OVER

No matter where he goes, people want to talk about it the instant they hear his name. And although Frank Reich has never been one to live in the past, he is more than happy to reminisce about that dank Buffalo day back in January of '93 when he engineered the greatest comeback in professional football history.

Just as Mike Eruzione will always be linked with the U.S. hockey team's "Miracle on Ice" at the 1980 Olympics, Reich will forever be tied to that wildcard game in which he quarterbacked the Buffalo Bills from a 32-point second-half deficit to a 41–38 overtime victory against the Houston Oilers.

Never mind that he spent 13 seasons in the National Football League and sparked some other pivotal wins during Buffalo's unprecedented string of four Super Bowls in the early 1990s. It was that one game that will always define Reich's career.

"I'm glad," he joked, "that people remember me for the comeback rather than the record three fumbles I had in one Super Bowl."

Of course, the way that game started, it appeared football historians would be remembering Warren Moon rather than Reich, who had started that day in place of the injured Jim Kelly. Moon turned in one of the most scintillating halves in playoff annals, completing an ungodly 19 of 22 passes for 218 yards and four scores before the Oilers headed to the visitors' locker room at Rich Stadium up 28–3.

Frank Reich looks to pass as he leads the Bills to one of the most amazing comebacks in NFL history, the 41–38 stunner over the Oilers on January 3, 1993, in Buffalo. Photo courtesy of Getty Images.

It appeared that the Bills' reign as two-time defending AFC champions was going to end in humiliating fashion. During intermission, in the deathly silent Bills locker room, special-teams star Steve Tasker leaned over and asked wide receiver Don Beebe in a whisper where they were going to play golf next weekend.

"It was said with thick sarcasm and disgust," Tasker recalled. "We weren't going golfing in January, so it was a joke, but we were in pretty big trouble. I mean, it was 28–3. But then we also said, 'Hey, we've been to two Super Bowls, we can't get embarrassed like this. Let's go out and battle in the second half, so when they look back five years later in the media guide and see we got beat 28–17 or something, it won't look so bad. We've got to do that. Let's get some self-respect back.'"

That was the brief message Bills Coach Marv Levy attempted to impart before his team headed through the tunnel for the third quarter.

"Did I think we still had a chance?" Levy said, reflecting on the moment. "Yeah, I suppose there was a glimmer of hope because there was so much time remaining. But it was about the same chance as you have of winning the New York State Lottery."

Kelly, sidelined with a concussion suffered in the regular-season-ending loss to these same Oilers the week before, tried to lighten the mood a bit.

"I told Frank, 'Well, you had the greatest comeback in college football history; let's see if you can do it in the pros,'" recalled Kelly, referring to the 1984 game when Reich led his Maryland Terrapins back from a 31–0 halftime deficit to defeat defending national champion Miami, 42–40.

"I was joking, but I guess Frank took me seriously."

Things, though, would get worse before they got better. Two minutes into the second half, cornerback Bubba McDowell picked off a Reich pass and raced 58 yards into the end zone to make it 35–3. Many in the crowd of 74,141 began packing up their stuff and heading

> ## DID YOU KNOW...
>
> That four Bills have been named MVP of the Pro Bowl? They are O.J. Simpson, Jim Kelly, Bruce Smith, and Steve Tasker.

for the exits. Reporters from the Houston press corps started making reservations for the following week's playoff game in Pittsburgh. The Buffalo media, meanwhile, started writing obituaries about the Bills' season.

But Reich's belief never wavered.

"It was 35–3, but remember what happened the previous week," he said, referring to the Oilers' 27–3 romp. "Now, it's 62–3 over the last six quarters, so how could you not let up? I'm not saying the Oilers were weak-minded, but it would be hard not to let down a little bit after dominating a team for six quarters and they did. Not a lot. It's not like they quit playing, but they opened the door just a little bit."

And the Bills came stampeding through.

Backup running back Kenneth Davis—playing in place of Thurman Thomas, who had left the game with a hip pointer just before McDowell's interception—capped a 50-yard drive with a one-yard plunge. On the ensuing kickoff, Steve Christie recovered his own onside kick, and Reich lofted a 38-yard touchdown pass down the left sideline to Beebe.

Suddenly, it was 35–17 with half of the third quarter remaining.

The Oilers went three-and-out, and Reich struck again—this time on a 26-yard touchdown toss to Andre Reed.

Following a Henry Jones interception, Reich found Reed again for an 18-yard score. And with 17 minutes left in regulation, the Bills had shaved the once-daunting deficit to just four points.

"The Oilers couldn't turn it back on," Tasker said. "When Frank hit Andre to make it 35–31, that game was over, and we were still down by four. We knew we were going to beat them. We couldn't stop. We were on fire. The defense was on fire and the crowd was insane."

So stirring was the comeback that many of the fans who had left attempted to scale the security fences to get back into the stadium.

Reich and Reed hooked up again from 17 yards to give Buffalo a 38–35 lead with 3:08 remaining in the game. Somehow, Houston regrouped long enough for Moon to march them 63 yards to set up the Al Del Greco field goal that sent the game into overtime.

"WHEN I TRY TO TAKE ON THE WEDGE, IT'S LIKE THROWING A MARSHMALLOW AT A STEAMROLLER."

—BILLS SPECIAL-TEAMS STAR STEVE TASKER

Suddenly, there was a distinct possibility that the great comeback might result in a great letdown, particularly after the Oilers won the coin toss before the extra session.

But on the third play of overtime, cornerback Nate Odomes intercepted a poorly thrown Moon pass and returned it to Houston's 20-yard line. Two plays later, Christie completed the memorable day with a game-winning 32-yard field goal.

There was shock and disbelief on both sides.

"It was the biggest choke in history," Houston cornerback Cris Dishman said after the game. "I think we have to put another word

DID YOU KNOW...

That Ralph Wilson offered the Bills head coaching job to Otto Graham before the team's first season in 1960, but the Hall of Fame quarterback turned it down, saying he was content to remain the athletic director at the Coast Guard Academy?

in the English dictionary to describe this loss because 'devastated' doesn't do it. Tell me I'm dreaming and this didn't happen."

It had. The Bills had won the lottery, and their backup quarterback proved he possessed—as the Rich Stadium banners boasted—"The Reich Stuff."

Though the Bills would go on to beat the Steelers in Pittsburgh and the Dolphins in Miami to win their third consecutive AFC title, they wound up being crushed 52–17 by Dallas in Super Bowl XXVII later that month.

And, yes, Reich wound up fumbling three times in relief of Kelly during that debacle, but no one ever brings that up.

"They'd much rather talk about the comeback game," said Reich, who became the president of the Reformed Theological Seminary in Charlotte, North Carolina, after his retirement from the game in 1998. "And that's fine with me."

OTHER COMEBACKS OF NOTE

Bills 45, Denver Broncos 38. Bears Stadium, Denver, October 28, 1962. Visiting Buffalo trailed 38–23 with 11:57 remaining, but stormed back behind quarterback Warren Rabb. He threw touchdown passes of 75 yards to Elbert Dubenion and 40 yards to Glenn Bass, then scored a game-tying two-point conversion. On the winning drive, Cookie Gilchrist took a short pass 74 yards to set up Rabb's winning touchdown on a three-yard run behind guard Billy Shaw's crunching block. "It's the greatest thrill I've ever had as a player and a coach," Bills Head Coach Lou Saban said after the game.

Bills 20, New York Jets 17. War Memorial Stadium, September 10, 1967. Buffalo scored 20 straight points in the fourth quarter. Mike Mercer, making his Bills debut, kicked a 43-yard field goal to win the game.

Bills 21, Oakland Raiders 20. Rich Stadium, September 16, 1974. Buffalo pulled out the *Monday Night Football* victory on Joe Ferguson's 13-yard touchdown pass to Ahmad Rashad with 26 seconds remaining. It was the Raiders' first loss in 13 *Monday Night Football* games.

Bills 20, New England Patriots 17. Rich Stadium, November 22, 1981. With only 35 seconds remaining, the Bills drove 73 yards in two plays and won the game when Joe Ferguson's 36-yard Hail Mary pass was deflected into the arms of Roland Hooks. The stadium was just one-fourth full when the play occurred.

Bills 23, Minnesota Vikings 22. Rich Stadium, September 16, 1982. The Bills rallied from a 19-point deficit to pull off a thrilling prime-time victory on a Thursday night. Ferguson hit Jerry Butler with an 11-yard touchdown pass for the win with 2:48 remaining.

Bills 38, Miami Dolphins 35 in overtime. Orange Bowl, Miami, October 9, 1983. Joe Ferguson completed 38 passes for 419 yards and Joe Danelo kicked the winning field goal.

Bills 34, Miami Dolphins 31 in overtime. Joe Robbie Stadium, Miami, October 25, 1987. The Bills battled back from a 21–0 deficit as Kelly completed 18 of 23 passes for 244 yards and two touchdowns in the second half and Robb Riddick scored three touchdowns. Scott Norwood's 27-yard field goal 4:12 into overtime decided it. "What are the odds of coming back from a 21-point

DID YOU KNOW...

That Joe Ferguson had 181 touchdown tosses and 190 interceptions as a Bill, while Jack Kemp had 77 scoring strikes and a whopping 132 interceptions during his Bills career? Fergy and Kemp are regarded as two of the best quarterbacks in Bills history, but you'd never know it by their touchdown-to-interception ratios.

deficit on the road against Dan Marino in his prime?" said former Bills general manager Bill Polian. "That victory was the turning point for us. That win and the manner in which it was accomplished made us believe in ourselves."

Bills 27, Miami Dolphins 24. Joe Robbie Stadium, Miami, September 10, 1989. Jim Kelly, who'll never be mistaken for an Olympic sprinter, fooled the Dolphins' defenders by running it in from the 2-yard line as time expired, capping a comeback from an 11-point deficit with about four minutes remaining.

Bills 23, Los Angeles Rams 20. Rich Stadium, October 16, 1989. Kelly was sidelined with a separated shoulder, but Frank Reich threw two touchdown passes in the final two minutes and 23 seconds to lead the underdog Bills to a stunning *Monday Night Football* victory against a Rams team that had brought a 5–0 record into the game.

Bills 29, Denver Broncos 28. Rich Stadium, September 30, 1990. Seventy-seven seconds—that's how long it took the Bills to score 20 points and wipe out a 21–9 fourth-quarter deficit. Nate Odomes started things when he blocked a David Treadwell field goal and Cornelius Bennett returned it 80 yards for a touchdown. On Denver's next possession, Leon Seals tipped a John Elway pass and Leonard Smith sprinted with it 39 yards for the score. Elway then fumbled a snap and Bennett recovered at the Broncos' 2-yard line, setting up Kenneth Davis's decisive score.

Bills 38, Los Angeles Raiders 24. Rich Stadium, October 7, 1990. The Bills trailed by three midway through the final quarter when Steve Tasker blocked a Jeff Gossett punt and J.D. Williams returned it 38 yards for the go-ahead score. Two plays later, Bennett caused a fumble, setting up a 23-yard field goal by Scott Norwood. Moments later, Odomes literally stole the ball from receiver Willie Gault and raced 49 yards for the touchdown.

Bills 23, New York Giants 20. Giants Stadium, East Rutherford, New Jersey, September 1, 1996. Buffalo rallied from a 17–0 deficit and won in overtime on Steve Christie's 34-yard field goal.

Bills 37, Indianapolis 35. Rich Stadium, September 21, 1997. Buffalo mounted the second-biggest comeback in NFL regular-season history, storming back from a 26–0 deficit. Rookie running back Antowain Smith capped the scoring frenzy with a 54-yard sprint to the end zone.

Bills 17, Jacksonville Jaguars 16. Rich Stadium, October 18, 1998. This was the game that ignited Buffalo's love affair with Doug Flutie. The diminutive quarterback scampered around left end on an improvised bootleg to score from the 1-yard line with 13 seconds remaining.

...AND SOME COMEDOWNS TO FORGET

Denver Broncos 38, Bills 38. Bears Stadium, Denver, November 27, 1960. Buffalo built a 38–7 lead in a blizzard, then collapsed and allowed the Broncos to score 31 unanswered points, including Gene Mingo's game-tying 19-yard field goal with nine seconds left.

Baltimore Colts 42, Bills 35. Rich Stadium, November 9, 1975. Buffalo was leading by 21 points in the second quarter, but the Colts staged a furious comeback behind Lydell Mitchell's three touchdowns.

Pittsburgh Steelers 30, Bills 24. Three Rivers Stadium, Pittsburgh, December 15, 1985. The Bills blew a 21–0 second-quarter lead and the Steelers staged the greatest comeback in their storied history.

St. Louis Rams 34, Bills 33. Rich Stadium, September 20, 1998. The Bills gave away an 18-point third-quarter lead and dropped to 0–3 for the first time in 13 seasons.

New York Jets 37, Bills 31. Ralph Wilson Stadium, September 9, 2002. Chad Morton shocked the Bills and ruined Drew Bledsoe's Buffalo debut by returning the opening kickoff in over-time 96 yards for a touchdown. Morton had also returned a kickoff for a score earlier in the game.

Miami Dolphins 24, Bills 23. Dolphins Stadium, Miami, December 4, 2005. In a game that ultimately marked the end of General Manager Tom Donahoe's reign in Buffalo, the Bills blew a 21-point lead. After J.P. Losman had thrown three touchdown passes in the first half, Coach Mike Mularkey became conservative, and the Dolphins stormed back for the win.

DREAM TEAMS

C hoosing an all-time Bills team can be as daunting as attempting to block Bruce Smith one-on-one on third-and-long. But we've decided to give it the old college try. Here's one man's starting lineup. Let the debating begin!

OFFENSE

Quarterback: Jim Kelly. I know, I know, even my grandmother could have picked this one, and she's been dead for 40 years. Jack Kemp and Joe Ferguson were good, but Kelly was superb. He holds virtually every career franchise passing record, including most attempts, completions, yards, and touchdowns. More importantly, he was 101–59 as a starter and guided the Bills to six AFC East titles and four consecutive Super Bowls, resuscitating a franchise that was about to bolt.

Running backs: O.J. Simpson and Thurman Thomas. Who's going to stop us with these two guys in the backfield? Simpson was the most electrifying player in team history—a home-run threat on every carry. Thomas didn't have Simpson's array of moves or his blazing speed, but he was a better pass receiver and blocker. The biggest problem for Kelly and the coaches would be deciding how to get each of these backs enough touches.

Some of the old-timers might argue for Cookie Gilchrist. I'd put him in there if we were going with a fullback. At 6'2", 243

Jim Kelly (left), Andre Reed (center), and Thurman Thomas are some of the most powerful offensive weapons the Bills ever had.

pounds, he could scatter would-be tacklers as if they were bowling pins, and when he was willing to block it was like having a pulling guard in your backfield. Plus, Cookie could kick extra points and once offered to play linebacker, too, if Ralph Wilson would double his salary.

For true fullbacks, you could also consider Jim Braxton or Sam Gash. Braxton was a better runner, once rumbling for close to 1,000 yards in a season, while Gash was primarily a blocker—twice making the Pro Bowl solely on his ability to open holes.

Wide receivers: Andre Reed and Eric Moulds. They rank first and second on the Bills' all-time receiving list, combining for 1,616 receptions, 22,191 yards, and 134 touchdown catches. Reed holds most of the franchise's major receiving records and will eventually be enshrined in Canton. Though Moulds wasn't a Hall of Famer, he established himself as the team's best offensive threat despite having to endure almost yearly changes at quarterback and offensive coordinator.

> ## "NO ONE EVER BLOCKED ME BETTER THAN JOE DeLAMIELLEURE."
>
> —STEELERS HALL OF FAME DEFENSIVE END "MEAN" JOE GREENE

The receivers behind these two are impressive. Elbert "Golden Wheels" Dubenion once averaged close to 30 yards per catch for a season. Bobby Chandler was a master at the acrobatic reception, especially along the sidelines. James Lofton is in the Hall of Fame, but spent the lion's share of his career elsewhere. Jerry Butler might have made it to the Hall of Fame, too, had it not been for injuries that short-circuited his career. And if we were to revisit this team a decade from now, current Bills go-to-guy Lee Evans might very well deserve the starting spot over Moulds.

Tight end: Pete Metzelaars. This hasn't been one of the franchise's stronger positions through the years. Metzelaars was a superb blocker and sure-handed receiver. What he lacked was a fifth gear. Still, despite possessing little speed, the 6'7", 250-pound redhead managed to make 302 catches for 2,921 yards and score 25 touchdowns during his 10 seasons with the team.

Ernie Warlick, a Canadian Football League import who played in the 1960s, averaged 17.2 yards per catch. And Jay Riemersma was also an offensive threat, with 204 catches, 2,304 yards, and 20 touchdowns.

Center: Kent Hull. One of Bill Polian's great diamond-in-the-rough discoveries. The Bills' general manager signed Hull to a deal shortly after the USFL folded, and the center went on to have a superb 11-year career. He earned three Pro Bowl invitations and was the quarterback of the offensive line during the Bills' Super Bowl years. That was no easy task; Buffalo was running the fast-paced no-huddle offense for much of that time, meaning he had to quickly read defensive front formations and make calls on the fly.

Al Bemiller also deserves consideration at the position. He played on Syracuse University's 1959 national championship squad and wound up in the middle of the Bills' offensive line for nine seasons.

Guards: Billy Shaw and Joe DeLamielleure. No debate here, as each of them has a bust in the Pro Football Hall of Fame. Shaw anchored the Bills' offensive line throughout the 1960s and played a pivotal role on Buffalo's AFL championship teams. Reggie McKenzie was a good player and a great quote, but Joe D was by far the superior lineman for the Bills' famous Electric Company. DeLamielleure was often out front on sweeps, leading the way for Simpson to break off big gainers. Joe D was also incredibly strong.

Ruben Brown and Jim Ritcher deserve consideration, too. Brown was an eight-time Pro Bowl selection and Ritcher was one of the strongest and most durable players in Bills history.

DID YOU KNOW...

That on September 1, 1991, Thurman Thomas became the first Bill to gain 100 yards rushing and receiving in the same game? Thomas carried the ball 25 times for 165 yards and a score—and caught eight passes for 103 yards and another touchdown—as Buffalo won a 35–31 shootout against Miami at Rich Stadium.

DID YOU KNOW...

That New York Jets/New England Patriots running back Curtis Martin is the all-time leading ground-gainer against the Bills, with 1,779 yards rushing? The only other opponents to crack the career 1,000-mark against Buffalo are Miami Dolphins great Larry Csonka, with 1,084, and former New England Patriot Sam Cunningham, with 1,072.

Tackles: Stew Barber and Joe Devlin. Barber teamed with Bemiller and Shaw to form the nucleus of the AFL's most dominating offensive line. Barber, who would later serve an unsuccessful stint as the team's general manager, earned All-League honors five times. Devlin was much less heralded but every bit as tough. A silent competitor who eschewed the spotlight, Devlin didn't earn a single Pro Bowl invitation during his 13 seasons with the team.

His lack of recognition was a mystery to teammates and opponents alike. "Joe Devlin is the toughest offensive tackle I've played against," said New York Jets star pass-rusher Mark Gastineau during the 1984 season, during which he set an NFL record for sacks with 22. "That he's never been picked as an All-Pro is an indictment of the selection process."

I give Devlin a slight edge over Will Wolford, a standout left tackle on the Bills' first three Super Bowl teams. Wolford earned two Pro Bowl invitations while protecting Kelly's blind side. He might have earned a starting nod on the Bills Dream Team had he spent more than seven seasons with them.

DEFENSE

Ends: Bruce Smith and Ron McDole. Smith is the greatest pass-rusher in team history with a record 171 sacks. He's also the NFL's all-time leader, having added to his total during several additional seasons with the Washington Redskins. When healthy and happy, the 6'4", 265-pound Smith could dismantle an offense all by his lonesome. McDole was a dancing bear, a 300-pounder in an era before linemen that size became commonplace. The Bills made a

Bruce Smith is known as one of the finest pass-rushers in the history of the NFL.

humongous mistake in 1970 when they traded him to the Redskins, where he turned in eight more productive seasons and earned a spot on Washington's all-time team.

Tackles: Tom Sestak and Fred Smerlas. A popular television commercial in the early 1980s asked: "Where's the beef?" On the Bills Dream Team roster, the beef can be found right here. These two bouncers made a living bench-pressing blockers and smothering ball carriers. Sestak was one of the most feared defensive players in the AFL, a guy who caused Hall of Fame quarterbacks such as Joe Namath and Len Dawson many a sleepless night. Smerlas earned five Pro Bowl invites and played more games at nose tackle than anyone in NFL history. The 6'4", 310-pounder was a linebacker's best

> "WHEN YOU PLAY AGAINST TOM SESTAK EVERY DAY IN PRACTICE, YOU EITHER IMPROVE OR RETIRE."
>
> —BILLY SHAW

friend, often tying up two blockers at a time so teammates Jim Haslett, Shane Nelson, and Shane Conlan would have a clear path to the running back.

Linebackers: Mike Stratton, Darryl Talley, and Cornelius Bennett. This might have been the most difficult unit of all to decide. You could take the corps of Stratton, Harry Jacobs, and John Tracey from the 1960s or Talley, Bennett, and Shane Conlan from the late 1980s

> # DID YOU KNOW...
>
> That Bruce Smith had a team-record 171 quarterback sacks during his 15 seasons with the Bills? That total included a single-season mark of 19 in 1990, one of eight seasons in which he reached double figures.

and early '90s and not go wrong. Stratton is best remembered for delivering the "hit heard 'round the world" against San Diego Chargers running back Keith Lincoln in the 1964 AFL championship game. But that was merely one of many brain-scrambling tackles he made during his 10-year Bills career, which saw him land a starting spot on the AFL's all-time team.

Bennett was one of the most dominating players in Bills history. Acquired during the famous Halloween Heist of 1987, Bennett was a superb pass-rusher who brought balanced pressure to the Bills' defensive front, preventing teams from ganging up on Smith. He finished his Bills career with five Pro Bowl selections, as well as the most fumble recoveries and fourth most sacks in team history.

Talley was one of the leaders of Buffalo's defense during its Super Bowl run. He might not have been as flashy or athletic as Bennett, but he was as tough and dependable as any player in Bills history.

"PLAYERS TODAY ARE TREATED LIKE ROYALTY. BACK THEN [THE 1960S], WE WERE JUST LOOKING FOR A JOB AND WERE SCARED TO DEATH OF GETTING CUT."

—FORMER BILLS WIDE RECEIVER AND SCOUT ELBERT DUBENION

DID YOU KNOW...

That Cornelius Bennett made 17 tackles, including four sacks, and forced three fumbles against the Philadelphia Eagles in a 17–7 loss in the 1987 season finale? You'd be hard-pressed to find a more dominating defensive performance than the one Bennett turned in that day. Afterward, Bills defensive coordinator Walt Corey told reporters: "They ought to put a film of that in a time capsule."

Cornerbacks: Butch Byrd and Robert James. Byrd was known for taking risks, and they usually paid off. Despite playing just seven seasons for the Bills, he intercepted 40 passes and returned five of them for touchdowns—franchise records that still stand. He was also an excellent punt returner. His 74-yard return of a punt for a touchdown in the second quarter of the 1965 AFL title game proved to be the backbreaker in a 23–0 shellacking of the San Diego Chargers.

James was discovered at tiny Fisk University in Tennessee by Bills receiver-turned-scout Elbert Dubenion. Though undersized, James could pack quite a wallop, and his sprinter's speed made him one of the best cover men in the game, as evidenced by his three consecutive Pro Bowl selections in the early 1970s.

> **"YOU BETTER GET SOMEBODY TO BLOCK FOR YOU ... OR I'M GOING TO KILL YOU TODAY."**
>
> —CORNELIUS BENNETT TO PHILADELPHIA EAGLES QUARTERBACK RANDALL CUNNINGHAM AFTER SACKING HIM FOR A FOURTH TIME DURING A 1987 GAME

Safeties: George Saimes and Steve Freeman. Saimes was one of three Bills to be named to the AFL's all-time team in 1969. Though he finished his career with 22 interceptions, he was best known for delivering hard hits from his strong safety position. Freeman was neither fast nor big, but he was extremely smart and durable. He picked off 23 passes during his 12 seasons with the Bills, returning three of the interceptions for touchdowns.

Arguments also could be made for Mark Kelso, with 30 interceptions, and Tony Greene, with 37.

SPECIAL TEAMS

Kicker: Steve Christie. In his nine seasons, Christie established himself as the Bills' all-time leading scorer, with 1,011 points. He also set records for most field goals in a game (6), season (33), and career (234). Signed to replace Scott Norwood following the 1991 season, Christie proved that his kicking leg was both accurate and powerful. In 1993 he booted a record 59-yarder—and a year later established yet another mark by converting 17 field goals in a row.

Punter: Brian Moorman. He's the Bills' version of Ray Guy, the old Oakland Raider who set the standard for NFL punters. Moorman earned consecutive Pro Bowl invitations in 2005 and 2006, booting his way into the Bills record book in the process. His average of 45.6 yards per kick in 2005 was the best in team history, and he's now supplanted Paul Maguire for best career average.

DID YOU KNOW...

That 39 players, including seven running backs, were selected ahead of Thurman Thomas in the 1988 NFL draft?

Kick coverer: Steve Tasker. No one has done it better, and if you don't believe me, then check with Deion Sanders or the voters who named Tasker to the NFL's 75th anniversary team. He was so dynamic while covering kickoffs and punts, or trying to block field goals and punts, that other teams actually game-planned for him.

If the seven-time Pro Bowl selection is the best special-teams player ever, then Mark Pike might just be the second-best. Despite his size (6'4", 265 pounds), Pike was an excellent open-field tackler and had a knack for getting down the field in a hurry.

Kick returner: Terrence McGee. Although he has only been with the Bills for four seasons, McGee has already established himself as the most prolific and dangerous kick returner in team annals. He already holds the marks for most returns, return yardage, and touchdowns (with four). Like Moorman, McGee is a game-breaker who plays an integral role in determining drive starts for his team.

Punt returner: Keith Moody. The former Syracuse University standout spent only four seasons in Buffalo, but that was long enough for him to earn a spot in our starting lineup. He averaged 10.5 yards per return during his career and took three back for scores.

COACHES

Head coach: Marv Levy. Who else but the Marvelous One? He guided the Bills to more wins than any other coach in team history, and is the only coach to take Buffalo to a Super Bowl. He was also the most intelligent and most humorous man to pace the Bills' sideline.

The Dream Team honorable mentions go to Lou Saban and Chuck Knox. Saban led the Bills to consecutive AFL championships in the mid-1960s and revived the team during his second stint with the Bills in the early 1970s. Knox did a similar rebuilding job in the late '70s and early '80s.

Offensive coordinator: Ted Marchibroda. Jim Kelly really began to flourish once Marchibroda came to town in 1987. The Bills experienced their most prolific scoring season in 1991 under Marchibroda, when they set franchise standards for points, with 458; total yards, with 6,252; and touchdown passes, with 39. It was Marchibroda who lobbied for Kelly to run the no-huddle offense after watching the quarterback tear apart the Cleveland Browns during a furious comeback that came up short in the January 1990 wild-card playoff game.

> **"IF YOU DID WHAT WE DID OUT ON THE STREET THEY'D PUT YOU IN A MENTAL WARD. ON THE FIELD, YOU CAN SPIT, CUSS, WIPE YOUR NOSE—WHATEVER—AND NOBODY NOTICES."**
>
> —LINEBACKER DARRYL TALLEY

Defensive coordinator: Joe Collier. He oversaw the miserly defenses that were the backbone of the Bills' back-to-back AFL titles, consistently shutting down the likes of Namath, Dawson, Hadl, and Blanda. His 1964 squad had a team-record 50 sacks, while his '65 unit forced a franchise-record 57 turnovers and allowed just 1,114 yards rushing.

Special-teams coach: Bruce DeHaven. During the Bills' Super Bowl run, their special teams were special, and DeHaven was a huge reason why. Under his guidance, they consistently ranked among the league leaders in fewest return yards allowed and were proficient at blocking punts, field goals, and extra points. Unfortunately, it was a special-teams play—Home Run Throwback in the 2000 AFC wildcard game against Tennessee—that ended DeHaven's 13-year career in Buffalo.

General manager: Bill Polian. The reasons are documented in greater detail in other areas of this book. Suffice it to say, Polian's fingerprints are all over those Super Bowl teams. An astute judge of talent, Polian turned a moribund franchise into champions through successful trades, drafts, and free-agent signings. But his biggest personnel decision wound up being the hiring of Levy as coach.

> ## "I GUESS THE VOTERS FINALLY LEARNED HOW TO SPELL MY NAME."
>
> —JOE DeLAMIELLEURE ON MAKING IT TO THE PRO FOOTBALL HALL OF FAME ON HIS 13th TRY

DO YOU KNOW THE WAY TO CANTON, OHIO?

On August 4, 2007, running back Thurman Thomas became the seventh Bill to be enshrined in the Professional Football Hall of Fame in Canton, Ohio. He joined O.J. Simpson, Billy Shaw, Marv Levy, Jim Kelly, Joe DeLamielleure, and James Lofton. And there are a few more Bills expected to receive busts in the coming years. Here's a look at who will get in, who should get in, and who's on the bubble.

Those Who Will Make It

Bruce Smith: The 11-time Pro Bowl player—and the NFL's all-time leader in quarterback sacks—is a mortal lock the instant he becomes eligible in a few years.

Andre Reed: Though he has superb numbers (941 receptions, 13,095 yards, 86 touchdowns, seven Pro Bowl invitations), Kelly's

ALL-TIME ROSTER

Offense

Number	Name	Position	Height	Weight	Years with Bills
88	Pete Metzelaars	TE	6'7"	245	1985–94
83	Andre Reed	WR	6'0"	195	1985–99
77	Stew Barber	T	6'2"	253	1961–69
66	Billy Shaw	G	6'2"	250	1961–69
67	Kent Hull	C	6'5"	275	1986–96
68	Joe DeLamielleure	G	6'3"	248	1973–79, 1985
70	Joe Devlin	T	6'5"	275	1976–82, 1984–89
80	Eric Moulds	WR	6'2"	210	1996–2005
12	Jim Kelly	QB	6'3"	220	1986–96
34	Thurman Thomas	RB	5'9"	205	1988–99
32	O.J. Simpson	RB	6'2"	205	1969–77

Defense

Number	Name	Position	Height	Weight	Years with Bills
78	Bruce Smith	DE	6'4"	265	1985–99
76	Fred Smerlas	DT	6'4"	295	1979–89
70	Tom Sestak	DT	6'4"	270	1962–68
72	Ron McDole	DE	6'4"	289	1963–70
58	Mike Stratton	LB	6'3"	237	1962–72
56	Darryl Talley	LB	6'4"	235	1983–94
97	Cornelius Bennett	LB	6'2"	236	1987–95
42	Butch Byrd	CB	6'0"	211	1964–70
20	Robert James	CB	5'10"	184	1969–74
26	George Saimes	SS	5'10"	195	1963–69
22	Steve Freeman	FS	5'11"	185	1975–86

Special Teams

Number	Name	Position	Height	Weight	Years with Bills
2	Steve Christie	K	6'1"	190	1992–2000
8	Brian Moorman	P	6'0"	175	2001–present
24	Terrence McGee	KR	5'9"	201	2003–present
46	Keith Moody	PR	5'11"	171	1976–79
89	Steve Tasker	KC	5'9"	180	1986–1997

favorite target has been passed over a couple of times by voters and may have to wait a few more years before receiving his due.

Bill Polian: The architect of the Bills' Super Bowl teams finally won his first Super Bowl ring in 2007 with the Indianapolis Colts. That should guarantee the five-time NFL Executive of the Year a spot in the Hall once he retires from his general manager's job in Indy.

Those Who Deserve to Make It

Steve Tasker: A seven-time Pro Bowl selection as a special-teams player, Tasker was named to the NFL's all-time squad a few years back. If he's good enough to be on the league's all-time team, he's good enough to have a bust in Canton.

Ralph Wilson: The only owner in Bills history was a major player in the merger of the AFL and NFL and has been described as "the conscience of pro football." Through the years, he's turned down several lucrative offers to move his franchise and has been a passionate advocate on behalf of the league's small-market teams. Some believe the voters have kept him out of the Hall because he played hardball with departed coach Wade Phillips and refused to put former coach Lou Saban on the Rich Stadium Wall of Fame.

Pete Gogolak: Yes, there have been better kickers, but Gogolak revolutionized the game with his soccer style. There should be a place in a Hall of Fame for trailblazers.

DID YOU KNOW...

That seven former Bills players went on to work as network broadcasters? They are Jim Kelly, Paul Maguire, Steve Tasker, Sam Wyche, Ray Bentley, Ronnie Pitts, Andre Reed, and James Lofton.

Bubble Guys

Fred Smerlas: A five-time Pro Bowl selection, Smerlas played more games than any nose tackle in football history. Though he doesn't have extraordinary stats, it's a tough position to measure because much of Smerlas's value was in tying up blockers so others could make plays.

Kent Hull: He earned only three Pro Bowl invites at center, but ask any Bill from the Super Bowl era and they'll tell you that Hull was every bit as important to the success of the no-huddle offense as Kelly, Thomas, or Reed.

Tom Sestak: Injuries cut short his career, and he didn't receive the exposure that many other AFL defensive stars did because the Bills didn't reach the Super Bowl during his tenure. But for a five-year span, Sestak was as dominating as any lineman in the league.

Darryl Talley: Although he received only two Pro Bowl invites and was overshadowed by flashier players like Smith and linebacker Cornelius Bennett, Talley was the heart and soul of those Super Bowl defenses. He may have been the most consistent and grittiest player on the team, but he is a long, long shot to ever make it to Canton.

Ruben Brown: He earned his ninth Pro Bowl bid during the 2006 season with the Chicago Bears. (His first eight came with the Bills.) Some believe that a few of those invites with the Bills were more on reputation than on performance. Like Talley, a long shot.

THE FIVE BEST TEAMS IN BILLS HISTORY

Year: 1990. Record: 13–3, first place AFC East, Super Bowl runner-up. Coach: Marv Levy. Details: After getting waxed 30–7 in Miami in the second game of the season, the Bills reeled off eight consecutive wins to capture the divisional title and home-field advantage throughout the playoffs. Jim Kelly, with 24 touchdown passes and a 101.2 rating, and Thurman Thomas, with 1,297 yards rushing and 532 receiving, keyed the innovative no-huddle offense. Bruce Smith had a franchise-record 19 sacks, and the Bills sent a record 10 players to the Pro Bowl. Frank Reich filled in admirably for the injured Kelly late in the season. The Bills outscored the Miami Dolphins and the Los Angeles Raiders 95–37 in the postseason, but wound up losing a 20–19 heartbreaker to the New York Giants in Super Bowl XXV.

Year: 1964. Record: 12–2, first place AFC East, AFL champions. Coach: Lou Saban. Details: Paced by the league's most miserly defense, the Bills opened their season with nine consecutive victories to win the AFL Eastern Division. Defensive tackle Tom Sestak had 14.5 sacks, Cookie Gilchrist rushed for 981 yards, and Elbert "Golden Wheels" Dubenion averaged 27 yards per catch and scored 10 touchdowns. The Bills limited opponents to just 65.2 yards rushing per game. They won their first American Football League championship by smothering the San Diego Chargers, 20–7.

THESE "WHEELS" WERE MADE FOR LONG HAULS

Elbert "Golden Wheels" Dubenion was one of the greatest deep threats in Bills history, and he was never more dangerous than in 1964, when he established a team record by averaging 27 yards per reception. Dubenion finished that season with 42 catches for 1,139 yards. The best day of his career came in a game against the New York Jets on October 24, 1964, when he snagged five balls for 218 yards. That season he also had huge games against the Boston Patriots, with three receptions for 127 yards, and the Houston Oilers, with five receptions for 183 yards. Add those three games and you get 13 receptions for 528 yards. That's more than 40 yards per catch.

Year: 1991. Record: 13–3, first place AFC East, Super Bowl runner-up. Coach: Marv Levy. Details: Kelly and league MVP Thomas each had their best seasons—Kelly with 33 touchdowns and 3,844 yards, and Thomas with 1,407 yards rushing and 631 receiving. Wide receivers Andre Reed and James Lofton each went over 1,000 yards receiving, and the Bills set a team scoring record with 458 points. The Bills' defense was not quite as intimidating as that of the '90 squad because Smith was sidelined with injuries much of the year. The unit, though, did come up big in the play-offs, particularly in a 10–7 victory against John Elway and the Denver Broncos in the AFC title game. But the Super Bowl futility continued as the Bills were dominated by a superior Washington Redskins team.

DID YOU KNOW...

That the only Bills to earn NFL Defensive Rookie of the Year honors are linebackers Jim Haslett, in 1979, and Shane Conlan, in 1987?

Year: 1965. Record: 10–3–1, first place AFC East, AFL champions. Coach: Lou Saban. Details: The Bills defense continued to lead the way, holding opponents to just 79.6 rushing yards per contest. Without Gilchrist, who had been traded, and Dubenion, who suffered a season-ending injury early on, more of the burden fell on Kemp. Although he finished with 10 touchdown passes and 18 interceptions, Kemp was voted the AFL's Most Valuable Player. The Chargers were favored in the league title-game rematch, but the Bills overpowered them again, 23–0, to win their second straight crown.

Year: 1980. Record: 11–5, first place AFC East, lost in the divisional round. Coach: Chuck Knox. Details: In just three seasons, Knox turned the 3–13 club he inherited into AFC East champions. Rookie running back Joe Cribbs did it all, rushing for 1,185 yards and 11 scores, and catching 52 passes. End Ben Williams (who had 12 sacks), Pro Bowl nose tackle Fred Smerlas, and linebackers Jim Haslett and Shane Nelson led a stout defense that picked off 24 passes and recovered 20 fumbles. The Bills had a Super Bowl–caliber team, but their quest fell short in a 20–14 loss to Dan Fouts and San Diego in the playoffs.

OUTSTANDING IN THEIR FIELD

THE SHORT, HEROIC LIFE OF ROBERT KALSU

Daddy,
    How I long for the day we will be together again. So many times I have wanted for you to put your arm around me, wipe a tear from my eye, or just laugh and tease with me. I think if we could be together we would be really close. I'm proud of you and the values you stood for. I love you.

—Jill Kalsu Horning in a note left at the
Vietnam Veterans Memorial in Washington, D.C.

Not a day goes by when they don't think about him. Not a day goes by when they don't wonder how different their lives might have been had a husband and a daddy not been taken from them in the prime of his life.

For more than three decades, the wife, daughter, and son of James Robert Kalsu have attempted to fill the huge void created by the Vietnam War. For more than three decades, they've been on a journey of discovery that has been profoundly gratifying and sad. For more than three decades, they have coped by remembering rather than forgetting.

"It's strange, but I feel as if I'm still getting to know my dad all these years later," said Jill Kalsu Horning, who was 18 months old when her father was killed on July 21, 1970, while coming to the aid of his troops at Firebase Ripcord on an isolated jungle hilltop in South Vietnam. "I keep learning more and more about him through the memories of people who knew him."

She paused to take a deep breath. She was doing her best not to cry on the other end of the phone line from her home in Oklahoma City.

"It makes me feel good to learn that he was a kindhearted, highly principled man—a true hero," she continued. "But it also makes me feel sad, somewhat cheated, that I didn't get to experience him for myself."

Some of those who did get to experience him were at Ralph Wilson Stadium on November 12, 2000, when Kalsu's name was added to the Bills Wall of Fame. Recognition of the only NFL player killed in Vietnam evoked powerful emotions among his widow, Jan, and their children, Jill and Bob Jr., who observed the unveiling from the field during ceremonies before the Bills played the Chicago Bears.

DID YOU KNOW...

That Joe Collier was the youngest Bills coach at age 33, and that Marv Levy was the oldest, taking over in 1986 at age 60?

"We can't thank the Bills enough for all they've done through the years to keep Bob's memory alive," said Kalsu's widow, Jan McLauchlin. "They didn't have to do any of this because he only played one season with them before going to Vietnam. To honor him this way warms our hearts, and means so much not only to us, but to all families who have lost loved ones to war."

Bob and Jan met on a blind date back in the autumn of 1966, when Bob was an All-American offensive guard at the University of Oklahoma and Jan was a sophomore at the nearby University of Central Oklahoma. They were both Catholic and deeply religious, and they hit it off immediately.

"You hear all those horror stories about blind dates, but we clicked from the moment we laid eyes on each other," Jan recalled. "Bob had this big ol' infectious smile and laugh that won you over. I remember going home after that first date and telling my sister, 'I think I met the man I'm going to marry.' That's how smitten I was."

Bob was smitten, too, and a year later, after he played the last game of his college football career

with the Sooners in the Orange Bowl, the two were married. When the Kalsus returned from their honeymoon, family members serenaded them at the Oklahoma City airport with strains of "Buffalo Gals, Won't You Come Out Tonight?"

"We didn't know at first why they were singing that song, but when they told us that Bob had been drafted by Buffalo, it all made sense," Jan said.

Other teams had been interested in Kalsu, too, but they shied away from him because they knew he had been an ROTC student at Oklahoma, and with the war raging in Southeast Asia, there was always the chance he might be called upon to fulfill his military obligations.

"That specter was always hanging over our heads, but we tried not to think about it," Jan said. "We were young and in love and everything seemed so wonderful in our lives."

That November, their lives became even more wonderful when Jill was born. Bob was overcome with joy. He spent every spare moment with his wife and daughter.

Professionally, things were going well, too. Though the Bills won only one of 14 games during the 1968 season, Kalsu broke into the starting lineup and was named the team's Rookie of the Year.

"Our life could not have been better," Jan said. "Then we got the call."

The army wanted Bob to trade in his blue Bills jersey for some green and brown combat fatigues. He was sent to Fort Still in Lawton, Oklahoma, for training. That September, while his Bills teammates prepared to open their season, Kalsu received orders that he was being shipped out to Vietnam as a second lieutenant in the 101st Screaming Eagles Airborne Division.

DID YOU KNOW...

That in a 51–24 rout of the Cincinnati Bengals on September 9, 1979, Roland Hooks scored four touchdowns on just five carries? He carried for three yards on a non-scoring play in the first half, then reached the end zone on runs of three, 32, four, and 28 yards after intermission.

"We couldn't stop crying when we got the news," Jan said. "Bob was the ultimate family man. He couldn't bear the thought of being away from me and Jill."

The next day, Jan visited her church and prayed. "I made a request of God," she recalled. "I said, 'If you must take Bob, then please give me a son.' After Bob left for Vietnam, I found out I was pregnant. Bob was so thrilled with the news. We both wanted to have a large family, and we were well on our way."

Bob wrote often; the letters were filled with love. He never mentioned the danger he and his troops were in. He didn't want to frighten her. But Jan couldn't help but be scared. She counted the days until they would meet again.

The reunion came in May 1970 when the army flew him to Hawaii for a week of R&R. Jan, seven months pregnant at the time, met him in Honolulu. She brought along Jill.

"When he ran off the bus from the airport, he was like a little kid," Jan said. "He couldn't wait to hug Jill. But the sight of this big guy barreling toward her frightened her. She clutched my legs and started to cry. Bob cried too, because he thought Jill had forgotten him. But she hadn't. I got her composed, and in no time she went back to being Daddy's little girl."

Jan couldn't help but notice how fatigued her husband was. He slept often that week. During one of his naps the hotel set off some fireworks, and Bob, mistaking the noise for gunfire, tore out of bed and sought cover.

"That was my first indication of how horrible the war must have been for him and his men," she said. "It shocked me."

The week passed much too fast. The departure was devastating. "He was running beside this tram that was taking Jill and me to the airport, and he was holding my hand," she recalled. "We were both crying. I said, 'Bob, please be careful,' and he said, 'No, Jan, you be careful; you're having our baby.' Then our grip broke. It was the last conversation we ever had, the last time we touched."

Roughly two months later, Bob was killed when mortar fire rained down on Ripcord. Less than 48 hours after his death, Jan gave birth to a baby boy. She couldn't wait to send Bob a letter telling him the news. But before she could set pen to paper, a teary-eyed soldier arrived at the hospital to inform her that her husband had been killed.

The next day, Jan changed her baby's name on the birth certificate to match her husband's: James Robert Kalsu.

Dad,

How I've missed the father-and-son things we could have done, the knowledge and love you could have given me. I can't wait for the time we are reunited to share our love and talk to each other. You are truly a person I can look up to.

I love you.

—Bob Kalsu Jr., in a note left at
the Vietnam Veterans Memorial

The years immediately following Bob's death were extremely difficult for Jan. At age 22, she was a widow with two children. Her deep religious faith and her family and in-laws helped sustain her.

From Day One, Jan was determined to make sure her children knew what a wonderful man their father was. "She wanted us to know as much as we could about Dad," Jill said. "She would tell us stories about him and encourage others to talk to us about him. It was really hard when we were younger because we yearned for him so badly even though we had no memories of him. But as time passed, I'm so glad Mom did that."

The void may have been toughest for Bob Jr. to fill. When he was a teenager, he wrote a gut-wrenching poem about missing his father, titled "Why God?"

It read in part:

Why my father, God?
What did he ever do?
You didn't even give him time
To tell his own son "I love you."
The love he showed for others
Could have been for me, too
Why him God?
Was he just for you?

Several years after Bob Jr. wrote that cathartic piece, Jan found a cassette tape her husband had sent home from Vietnam just before he was killed. She played it for her children. The recording finished with these words to his unborn son: "And now for you, Baby K, Daddy loves you and pretty soon I'll be home to hold you."

Both Jill and Bob Jr. are now parents themselves in their mid-thirties. Jill is a teacher and her brother is an attorney. Both live in the Oklahoma City area, not far from their mom and stepfather, Bob McLauchlin, whom Jan married in 1985.

Jill and Bob Jr. intend to pass along the stories they've heard about their father to their children. They will make family trips to the Pro Football Hall of Fame in Canton, Ohio, where there is a display dedicated to Kalsu, and to Ralph Wilson Stadium, where his name will be prominently displayed for as long as professional football is played there. They will teach their children that their grandfather was a kindhearted man, a man of his word, and a true hero who made the ultimate sacrifice.

DID YOU KNOW...

That the Bills picked off 38 of Pro Football Hall of Famer George Blanda's passes, including six in a contest on September 9, 1962?

"During those rare breaks from chasing his grandchildren around, I'll sit and think about how nice it would be to have him here, just to chew the fat with him," Jill said. "The nice thing is that even though my brother and I have no memories of him, we feel as if we know him, thanks to my mom and others. We feel as if he has been with us in spirit throughout our lives."

My prayer, my dear and sweet husband, is that the world would forever know peace so that never again will death separate and permanently sear the hearts of families torn by the tragedies of war. I await the day when the Lord reunites us in heaven. Honey, I love you forever.

—Note left by Jan Kalsu at
the Vietnam Veterans Memorial

VANDEMONIUM IN BUFFALO

Van Miller's play-by-play career began long before he sat in front of his first microphone. As a 10-year-old growing up in Dunkirk, New York, just a Brian Moorman punt or two north of the Pennsylvania border, Miller prepped for his life's work by broadcasting fictitious Notre Dame football games into a hose, an eggbeater, or a spoon.

"I must have called about 150 of the Fighting Irish's games for an audience of one—me," said the voice of the Buffalo Bills. "And you know what? Notre Dame won every one of those games I broadcast. They were undefeated with me at the mike."

Although the Bills weren't as successful as Van's make-believe Irish teams, they did have their moments. And they were blessed to have had Miller as their soundtrack for nearly four decades. Like a favorite uncle, he was a welcome visitor to fans' homes on Sundays in the fall, painting compelling, occasionally humorous word pictures of the team western New York followed with religious fervor.

Vandemonium, the longest-running radio play-by-play show in National Football League history, lasted for 37 seasons. The beloved Bills announcer asked fans to "fasten their seat belts" for

Van Miller calls a Bills game against the Miami Dolphins on December 21, 2003. It was Miller's last season, ending what he referred to as a 37-year "labor of love" as the Bills' play-by-play announcer, the longest tenure with a single team in NFL history.

one last ride with him when he called Buffalo's 2003 season finale in Foxboro, Massachusetts, against the New England Patriots.

Miller was to the Bills what Harry Caray was to the Cubs, Mel Allen was to the Yankees, and Chick Hearn was to the Lakers. You heard Miller speak and you immediately thought Buffalo Bills. It didn't matter if he was pitching cellular phones or telling one of his 10,000-plus jokes; broadcaster and team were joined at the vocal cords.

Whether describing the euphoria of the greatest comeback in NFL history or the bitter disappointment of Scott Norwood's wide-right field goal attempt in the waning moments of Super Bowl XXV, Miller had always been, in the words of NFL Films President Steve Sabol, "an announcer able to deliver the moment."

The Patriots game was his 752nd Bills broadcast (that total includes exhibition and postseason games). It brought his illustrious career full circle.

"My first game was an exhibition against the Boston Patriots on July 30, 1960," Miller said on the eve of his final broadcast. "They were coached by future Bills coach Lou Saban, and they beat the Buster Ramsey–led Bills, 28–7. Now I'm wrapping it up against the Patriots. I guess what goes around comes around."

Miller would have worked every single game in franchise history, but there was a brief span in the early 1970s when his station lost the broadcast rights.

"That stretch when he was gone, something definitely was missing; there was a void," said John Murphy, who grew up in suburban Buffalo idolizing Miller and worked as his color man for 16 years.

"I remember going to a Bills game with my friend [current Michigan basketball coach John Beilein] in 1979, and it just happened to be Van's first game back. We're listening to the action on the radio, and John turns to me and says, 'You know, Murph, that's what Bills football sounds like.' And he was right. So many of us grew up with that voice and this football team. It's like Van's a member of every fan's family."

DID YOU KNOW...

That Van Miller's 37 years as the "Voice of the Bills" is the longest run by any team broadcaster in NFL history?

Miller was born in Buffalo but raised in the Chautauqua County town of Dunkirk, about an hour south of Ralph Wilson Stadium. His father abandoned his family when Miller was a baby, and he was raised by his mom, Esther.

"My mom never bad-mouthed him about that or about the fact he left us," Miller said. "She just put her nose to the grindstone and assumed the role of mother and father. It wasn't easy back then working a full-time job and raising a child by yourself, but she did it with flying colors. She made sure I never went without. I called her the Iron Lady because she was so mentally and emotionally strong."

Miller's tight bond with his mom was one of the reasons he later spurned offers from the networks. He didn't want to leave western New York and be far away from the woman who helped him realize his dreams.

Miller's promising athletic career came to an end when he broke his back in a bus accident while returning from Syracuse University following his freshman year. Radio gave him an opportunity to stay involved in sports. He got his start in the business at his hometown station of WFCB-AM.

DID YOU KNOW...

That neither the Bills nor the San Francisco 49ers punted during their game on September 13, 1992?

"I had listened to the guy who was doing the play-by-play of Dunkirk high school basketball games, and he was just awful," Miller said. "So I decided to do something bold. I walked into the station and told the owner that he needed a play-by-play man like me. I did a demo for him and in it I had him throwing in a 30-footer to win the game. He was impressed that I had used his name, and he said the job was mine for $10 a game."

A few years later, Miller met his wife, Gloria, who was a student and a baton twirler at Fredonia State. They've been inseparable ever since.

At WFCB, Miller was literally a Van for all seasons. He did every sport imaginable, from soapbox derby races to wrestling matches featuring the likes of Gorgeous George and the Great Togo.

"I've got to be the only living broadcaster who has done Super Bowls and wrestling on radio," Miller quipped.

In addition to describing the wrestling action, Miller also served as a ring announcer at matches. One night, he unwittingly became part of the action after Gorgeous George put his clammy hand on Van's gaudy, cream-colored jacket.

"He left a big mark on it, so I told him he was going to have to pay to get it dry-cleaned," Miller said. "Well, he didn't take too kindly to that. He was really insulted. He looked down at me and called me a peasant. Fortunately, that's as far as it went. He was a big guy and if he had wanted to, he could have tossed me around like a rag doll."

Miller also ventured outside sports, hosting the *Van the Morning Man Show*, as well as the *Polish Hour*, academic quizzes, and big-band performances live.

"I even did news and weather," he said. "Saturdays in the fall I was on the go from six in the morning to midnight. But I was young and it was a great training ground."

In 1955 Miller headed up the road to Buffalo and landed an announcer's job at WBEN-AM. It was supposed to be a temporary gig, but it wound up lasting four decades.

He broadcast Bisons baseball when Johnny Bench was a hot prospect, the Braves' National Basketball Association games during the "Ernie D" and "McAdoo Can Do" era, and Niagara basketball teams led by scoring machine Calvin Murphy.

But his biggest break came in 1960 when Dick Gallagher, the Bills' first general manager, told team owner Ralph Wilson: "We have to get this guy Miller to do our games." It was the beginning of a beautiful relationship between announcer, owner, and team.

"It's probably one of the best personnel decisions we've ever made," said Wilson, who often played tennis against Miller and once gave the announcer an all-expenses-paid trip to Wimbledon. "Van has done as much to spread the word of Bills football and contribute to their popularity as anyone. Players come and players go, but Van's been our constant."

Pressed to pick his most memorable game, Miller went with the

> ## DID YOU KNOW...
>
> That the Bills scored 31 points in the first quarter in the 1964 season opener against the Kansas City Chiefs?

Bills' comeback from a 32-point deficit in that 1993 playoff game against the Houston Oilers.

"In my heart, I thought the game was over before halftime. But as a broadcaster, you have to continue to describe the action to the bitter end, and that can be tough," he said. "I don't think that comeback will ever be duplicated. It's like Joe DiMaggio's 56-game hitting streak; it's untouchable."

Yes, the four consecutive Super Bowl losses were painful, but Miller managed to keep things in perspective. "You can look back and say that Super Bowl XXV was the one that got away, but you can't ever lose sight of the fact that these are only games," he said. "I love the excitement and drama of the games, and I get caught up in the action. But let's be real. I mean, we've got soldiers being killed in Iraq. Football is entertainment. It's not war."

One of Miller's greatest assets was his sense of humor and his ability to tell stories. Through the years, he worked with a one-eyed spotter and a drunken one, too.

"The guy had gotten into the martinis at a pre-game party, and he was half in the bag by the time the game kicked off," Miller said. "Early in the game, there's this holding call against the Bills that negated a long gain and the guy starts going ballistic in the booth. He's leaning out the window and screaming at the ref. He said some choice words that our listeners had to hear over the airwaves. They were words that the FCC doesn't like to hear."

Some criticized Miller in his latter years. They said he was a step behind the play and too reliant on Murphy and the spotters. Miller admitted his eyesight wasn't quite what it had been, and that contributed to his decision to retire when he did.

"The bottom line, though, is that I've done this for 37 years and I felt it was time to make the move," he said. "I have no regrets. It's been a fantastic ride for me."

And a fantastic ride for Bills fans, too.

REPRESENTATIVE JACK KEMP PLAYS POLITICAL FOOTBALL

Jack Kemp went from running for daylight to running for political office. He graduated from old War Memorial Stadium, to the U.S. House of Representatives, to President Reagan's cabinet. Kemp's post-football career path didn't surprise his former Bills teammates in the least. They just can't believe the quarterback's journey didn't take him all the way to the White House.

"I think," said Bills owner Ralph Wilson, "he would have made a hell of a quarterback for the country."

Billy Shaw, an All-League guard who once protected Kemp from would-be tacklers,

> "PRO FOOTBALL GAVE ME A GOOD PERSPECTIVE WHEN I ENTERED THE POLITICAL ARENA. I HAD ALREADY BEEN BOOED, CHEERED, CUT, SOLD, TRADED, AND HUNG IN EFFIGY."
>
> —JACK KEMP, BILLS QUARTERBACK

vividly remembers the quarterback campaigning locker-to-locker for Republican presidential candidate Barry Goldwater (who was running against Lyndon Johnson) before the 1964 election.

"Jack stopped by my stall for about half an hour extolling the virtues of Goldwater," recalled Shaw, a member of the Pro Football Hall of Fame. "Now, I don't remember the particulars of his spiel, but I do remember him being quite convincing. He got me to vote for Barry."

While many of his teammates restricted their reading to the playbook and *Playboy*, Kemp was devouring books such as Edward Gibbon's *The History of the Decline and Fall of the Roman Empire* or John Maynard Keynes's *The General Theory of Employment, Interest, and Money*.

"I used to kid Jack that carrying those big books on the plane was part of his weight-lifting routine," said Eddie Abramoski, the Bills' longtime trainer. "Jack often would give me one of the books and say, 'Abe, you should read this. This is what's wrong with our country.' Or, 'This is the direction we should be going.' Eventually,

DID YOU KNOW...

That despite finishing with 18 interceptions and a 54.8 pass efficiency rating, Jack Kemp earned American Football League Most Valuable Player honors in 1965?

the conversations always got around to politics. Jack was passionate about it."

Kemp was equally passionate about football. His arrival in Buffalo during the 1962 season marked a turning point in Bills history. Lou Saban had taken over as head coach that fall, and had begun assembling the defensive players who would form the backbone of the Bills' championship teams of the mid-1960s.

"The missing piece was the quarterback," said Bills owner Ralph Wilson. "That's why, when Jack became available, we spent about two seconds deliberating before claiming him off the waiver wires [from the San Diego Chargers]. Our defense was good enough to make us contenders, but you've got to have a quarterback, a leader, if you want to win a championship."

Kemp paid immediate dividends, helping the Bills overcome an 0–5 start to finish 7–6–1. The following season, they made the playoffs but were beaten by the Boston Patriots. In 1964, the Bills went 12–2 and won their first AFL title. They repeated in 1965, and Kemp earned league MVP honors.

DID YOU KNOW...

That Jack Kemp established the team standard for most touchdowns by a quarterback when he rushed for eight scores in 1963?

Although he finished as the AFL's all-time passing-yardage leader and competed in five title games in 10 years, Kemp's time in Buffalo was not without its difficult moments. Saban occasionally played musical quarterbacks, yanking Kemp and putting in popular backup Daryle Lamonica. The relationship between Kemp and Saban was mostly a good one, but there were times when the strong wills of quarterback and coach clashed.

"Jack wasn't afraid to stand tall for what he believed in, and sometimes when he didn't agree with a play Lou sent in, he would run his own," Shaw said. "If the play worked, Lou was fine. If the play didn't work, Lou would send in Lamonica."

The occasional benchings were difficult for Kemp to stomach, but he never complained.

LIVES AFTER FOOTBALL

Jack Kemp wasn't the only former Bills player to pursue a political career after his playing days. One of his teammates, Ed Rutkowski, wound up becoming county executive of Erie County, and Walt Patulski, the Bills' number one draft pick in 1972, spent time as the Commissioner of the Board of Education in Syracuse, New York.

Before being accused of double murder in 1994, O.J. Simpson achieved fame and fortune as a pitchman for Hertz Rental Car, as a network football broadcaster, and as a mediocre actor in numerous movies, including the popular *Naked Gun* series.

Offensive guard Jim Ritcher may have chosen the most interesting second career. He became a commercial airline pilot.

Interestingly, several former Bills wound up landing network broadcasting jobs. Among them are Paul Maguire, Steve Tasker, Jim Kelly, Ray Bentley, James Lofton, Sam Wyche, Ronnie Pitts, and Andre Reed.

"I roomed with him, and if he were upset about it, I'm sure he would have said something to me," Shaw said. "I know if it were me in that situation, I'd have a tough time keeping my feelings to myself. But that was Jack. He was a true team player."

Kemp was often the target of fan criticism. He has joked that his job as quarterback of the Bills prepared him for a career in politics because he had already been booed, spit on, and hung in effigy.

"I guess it did thicken his skin," Shaw said. "But I know it bothered him, and a lot of it was unfair. Jack would get blamed for the missed blocks and the wrong routes and dropped passes. But just like with the quarterback controversy, he kept it to himself. That's part of being a leader, putting the team above yourself."

Kemp, who helped co-found the AFL players' union in 1965, was the go-to guy when his teammates had gripes with the coaching staff. In his most famous mediation, Kemp convinced Saban to allow star running back Cookie Gilchrist back on the team after the coach had released him for insubordination in November 1964.

"Jack was a master at solving problems without confrontation," said former Bills cornerback Booker Edgerson. "He told Lou that the entire team wanted Cookie back because it was best for the team, and since it was a team decision, Lou agreed. But Jack helped make it happen because I believe Lou had great respect for him."

> **"WE KNEW [JACK KEMP] WAS SCARED TO DEATH WHEN HE WENT UNDER THE GUARD FOR THE SNAP."**
>
> —BILLY SHAW

The voters of western New York also had that respect for him, sending him to Congress for nine consecutive terms. Kemp spent time in the Reagan administration as the director of the department of Housing and Urban Development, and was Republican Bob Dole's running mate in the 1996 presidential election. They wound up losing decisively to Bill Clinton and Al Gore.

THE BILLS' BIGGEST BACKER

On the desk at Chris Berman's office at ESPN headquarters in Bristol, Connecticut, you will find a piece of the Rich Stadium goal posts that came down after the Bills clinched the AFC East title in 1988. It was sent to him by several admiring fans who appreciate the manic, nickname-spouting sports anchor's undying loyalty to western New York's favorite team.

"It's been a hell of a ride," said Berman of his bond with the Bills. "It started back in the summer of '88. I was traveling from training camp to training camp, and when I showed up at Fredonia, I had this real good feeling about the team. The Bills had gone 7–8 the year before, and I just sensed that things were in place for them to take off. On *SportsCenter*, I started building them up, and they made me look good every week.

"I think the special relationship I've had with the Bills was due in part to my closeness in age to many of the players from their Super Bowl run. I was 33 at the time, and most of the key players on the Bills were in their mid-to-late twenties. It's like we grew up together."

Berman's admiration for the Bills actually began in his youth. He grew up in the New York City area in the 1950s and '60s, and although the Joe Namath–led Jets were his favorite team, he developed a fondness for several other old American Football League clubs, including the Bills.

"They had a bruising defense and they always played Joe Willie tough," he said. "I respected them when they had Kemp and Fergy and the Juice and Chuck Knox and the Bermuda Triangle. And I respect them now."

His ESPN colleagues occasionally razz him, and viewers sometimes voice their displeasure, but Berman said most people are good sports about his Bills boosterism.

"People know that I'm never putting down their team," he said. "I just like talking about the Bills. And I think they deserved to be talked about prominently, given what they accomplished. I think history will look kindly on them."

Twice, Berman has been awarded the key to the city of Buffalo. Some zealots have even suggested his name be placed on the Ralph Wilson Stadium Wall of Fame, alongside Kelly, Kemp, and DeLamielleure.

"Even though I hope to be in this business another 25 years, I doubt I'll ever develop a bond with a team like I had with this one," he said of the Super Bowl Bills. "Some of it is just an age thing. I'm not going to be that close in age to a group of players again. It was just a special time for me as a journalist."

DID YOU KNOW...

That Jan Stenerud of the Kansas City Chiefs kicked 10 field goals in two games against the Bills during the 1969 season?

The sportscaster known as Boomer is one of several national celebrities who have pulled for the Bills. Tim Russert of NBC's *Meet the Press* is a Buffalo native who never hides the fact he bleeds blue-and-red. Other Bills fans include Donald Trump, Supreme Court justice John Roberts, golfer Phil Mickelson, comic writer Nick Bakay, and rock stars Meat Loaf and Eddie Van Halen.

WHAT'S IN A (NICK)NAME?

As a charter member of the National Football League in 1920, Buffalo was known as the All-Americans. The team later switched its name to the Bisons, then the Rangers, before dropping out of the NFL following the 1929 season.

When pro football returned to the Queen City in 1946, Buffalo's entry in the fledgling All-American Football Conference once again became known as the Bisons. But team owner Jim Breuil didn't care for the name, so before the 1947 season, he held a name-the-team contest.

One of the contestants, a man named Jimmy Dyson, suggested "Bills" after Buffalo Bill Cody, the famous 19th century frontiersman. Dyson reasoned that the name was appropriate because Breuil's Frontier Oil company was sponsoring the team, and Buffalo was exploring a sports frontier of sorts with its new football franchise. Breuil liked the suggestion, and Dyson was presented with a check for $500.

Sadly, the league ceased operations in 1950, and despite solid fan support, Buffalo wasn't one of the AAFC teams absorbed by the established National Football League.

When it was announced nine years later that Buffalo would be joining the new American Football League, the *Buffalo Evening News* held another name-the-team contest. About a thousand ballots were returned to the newspaper and scores of names were

---

DID YOU KNOW...

That guard Mitch Frerotte, also known as the "Pit Bull," was a secret weapon in goal-line situations, catching two passes for scores? Tackles John Fina and Jason Peters are other offensive linemen who have caught touchdown passes for the Bills.

---

suggested. Among them: Bruisers, Bees, Marauders, Condors, Bombers, Brutes, Bucks, Eries, and Red Jackets. One clever person even proposed naming them the Wils after Ralph Wilson, the Detroit businessman who was bringing professional football back to western New York.

The majority, though, cast their ballots for the Buffalo Bills, and Wilson, not one to buck tradition, gladly went along with public sentiment.

"The old team was a proud team," he said of Buffalo's AAFC franchise. "Its fans had been very loyal. I could not see any reason why we should change the name."

Nicknames are commonplace in sports, and the Bills have had their share of colorful ones through the years. The offensive line that turned the Juice (O.J. Simpson) loose became known as the Electric Company, after a popular Saturday morning cartoon.

Mike Dodd, a former Buffalo newspaper reporter who now writes for *USA Today*, coined the moniker "The Bermuda Triangle" for the defensive trio of nose tackle Fred Smerlas and inside linebackers Jim Haslett and Shane Nelson. Dodd's nickname worked—the Bills' Bermuda Triangle was a place where running backs disappeared.

DID YOU KNOW...

That Daryle Lamonica averaged a team-record 8.88 yards per attempt in 1964? The "Mad Bomber" loved throwing deep, and it paid off.

BILLS NICKNAMES THROUGH THE YEARS

Here's a look at some of the more clever Bills sobriquets:

Nickname	Real Name
Golden Wheels	Elbert Dubenion
Cookie	Carlton Gilchrist
Juice	O.J. Simpson
Pit Bull	Mitch Frerotte
The House	Howard Ballard
Biscuit	Cornelius Bennett
The Rockpile	War Memorial Stadium
The Ralph	Ralph Wilson Stadium
Machine Gun Kelly	Jim Kelly
Hammerhead, Jughead, Buckethead	Shane Conlan
The Electric Company	The Bills' offensive line of the early 1970s, featuring guards Joe DeLamielleure and Reggie McKenzie, centers Bruce Jarvis and Mike Montler, tackles Donnie Green and Dave Foley, and tight end Paul Seymour
Squatty Body, the Thurmanator	Thurman Thomas
The Mad Bomber	Daryle Lamonica
Absorba the Greek	Fred Smerlas
Seve	Steve Tasker
Dr. Sack	Leon Seals
The Texas Twister	Kenneth Davis
The Baby-Faced Assassin	Harry Jacobs
Bootin' Tuten	Rick Tuten
Go-Go	Pete Gogolak
The Sultan of Sayonara	Lou Saban
Thunder Thighs	Ira Albright
The Dancing Bear	Ron McDole
Joe D	Joe DeLamielleure and Joe Devlin

Nickname	Real Name
Bubby	Jim Braxton
Mr. Peepers	Mark Kelso
The General	Marvcus Patton
Ground Chuck	Coach Chuck Knox's ground-oriented offense
Fergy	Joe Ferguson
Wazoo	Dudley Meredith
Abe	Eddie Abramoski
Earthquake Enyart	Bill Enyart
Marlin the Magician	Marlin Briscoe
Darby the Dinosaur	Ray Bentley
Big Hoss	Ernie Warlick
Crawfish	Paul Guidry
Killer	Keith McKeller
Brew	Larry Kinnebrew
The Wabash Cannonball	Pete Metzelaars
Playmaker	Nate Clements
Talley Whacker	Darryl Talley
Tippy	Tom Day

NOMADIC LOU

He guided the Buffalo Bills to back-to-back American Football League championships in the mid-1960s and is credited with salvaging O.J. Simpson's career during his second coaching stint with the team in the early 1970s.

But Lou Saban is best known for something else—his disappearing acts. Few sports figures can boast a resume or a travel log as cluttered as Saban's. If he had a business card, it would surely read: HAVE WHISTLE, WILL TRAVEL.

It's no mystery why the second-winningest coach in Bills history has been called the "Sultan of Sayonara" and "the Marco Polo of coaching." Since his first sports job as an undersized but hard-nosed linebacker for the Cleveland Browns in 1946, the nomadic Saban has barely stayed in any one place long enough to allow his mail to catch up to him.

Lou Saban (left) lets out a cheer with three of his top players in the Bills' dressing room after winning the AFL Championship on December 26, 1964. Shown from left are Pete Gogolak, Jack Kemp, and Wray Carlton.

He has coached football on virtually every level—high school, college, semipro, and pro—and has also served as president of the New York Yankees, sold insurance, and run a horse-racing track. Since his final season as a player in 1949, Saban has held 30 different jobs in a 53-year span. His longest stay: five years as head football coach at a junior college in Canton, New York. His shortest stay: 19 days as athletics director at the University of Cincinnati.

Some believe his wandering ways can be traced to his ethnicity. See, Saban is Croatian, and the Croats, throughout their history, have been persecuted and forced to live a nomadic existence in search of a homeland.

Saban's dad, Nikola, was well traveled, too. He immigrated to America in 1912 and worked several mining jobs throughout the United States before finally settling in the Chicago area.

As a boy, Lou helped the family make ends meet by caddying for the brother of gangster Al Capone at local golf courses. At age

15, Lou joined the mining company where his father worked, helping to dig the subways of the Windy City. That project took years to complete, and when it was done, Nikola hit the road again in search of work. It was a pattern his son would follow.

Coaching has always been Lou's first love, especially at the collegiate level. Saban is credited with helping revive the University of Miami football program. (His two most famous recruits were quarterback Jim Kelly and running back Ottis

> **"I CAN'T BELIEVE LOU QUIT ON ME AGAIN."**
> —RALPH WILSON AFTER SABAN RESIGNED IN MIDSEASON JUST TWO DAYS BEFORE A GAME WITH THE COLTS IN BALTIMORE

Anderson, who, in a fateful twist, wound up winning MVP honors in the Giants' upset of the Bills in Super Bowl XXV.)

Saban and football legend John Heisman are the only men in history who have been head coaches at eight different colleges.

Saban's last job (at least we think it was his last job) was head football coach of Chowan College, a Division III program in North Carolina, in 2002. He was 81 years old that fall.

His record of 70 wins, 47 losses, and four ties ranks second only to Marv Levy on the Bills' all-time list. Despite being one of the most prominent figures in team history, Saban's name has not been affixed to the Wall of Fame at Ralph Wilson Stadium. Wilson, the team's owner since its inception, adamantly refuses to honor Saban because he feels as if the coach quit on him twice. In a 2004 interview, Saban said he doesn't lose sleep over the exclusion.

"It would be quite an honor, but I understand the reasons," he said.

Wilson is hardly the only person to have been upset by Saban through the years. When Lou left the Hurricanes in 1979 after just

---

DID YOU KNOW...

That kicker John Leypoldt learned of his release from the team while listening to Coach Lou Saban's postgame radio show?

LOU SABAN'S RESUME

- 2001–2002: Head football coach, Chowan College (North Carolina)
- 1995–2000: Head football coach, SUNY-Canton College of Technology
- 1994: Head football coach and development officer, Alfred State College (New York)
- 1994: Head coach, Milwaukee Mustangs (Arena Football League)
- 1992: Head coach, Tampa Bay Storm (Arena Football League)
- 1991: Head football coach, Peru State College (Nebraska)
- 1990: Head coach, Middle Georgia Heatwave (semipro football)
- 1989: Head football coach, Georgetown High School (South Carolina)
- 1988: Head football coach, South Fork High School (Stuart, Florida)
- 1986–87: Assistant football coach, Martin County High School (Stuart, Florida)
- 1984–86: Consultant and scout, New York Yankees
- 1983–84: Head football coach, University of Central Florida
- 1981–82: President, New York Yankees
- 1980: Executive assistant, Tampa Downs Raceway
- 1979: Head football coach, U.S. Military Academy, West Point, New York
- 1977–78: Head football coach and athletic director, University of Miami (Florida)
- 1976: Athletic director, University of Cincinnati
- 1972–76: Head coach, Buffalo Bills
- 1967–71: Head coach, Denver Broncos
- 1966: Head football coach, University of Maryland
- 1962–65: Head coach, Buffalo Bills
- 1961: Scout and pro personnel director, Buffalo Bills
- 1960–61: Head coach, Boston Patriots
- 1957–59: Head football coach, Western Illinois University
- 1956: Insurance sales agent, Mutual Benefit, Chicago, Illinois
- 1955: Head football coach, Northwestern University
- 1954: Assistant football coach, Northwestern University
- 1953: Assistant football coach, University of Washington
- 1950–52: Head football coach, Case Institute (now Case Western Reserve), Cleveland, Ohio
- 1946–49: Linebacker, Cleveland Browns, All-American Football Conference

two seasons to take the head football job at the U.S. Military Academy, respected *Miami Herald* columnist Edwin Pope had this venomous response:

> "If he wants to quit on himself, as now appears to be a proven pattern, that can be excused. But quitting after two years on a school that believed in him enough to hand him a six-year contract at 55 is something else. You want a deserter, Army? You got one."

There were those, though, who swore by him rather than at him. He had a knack for resurrecting moribund football programs and getting the most out of his players, especially running backs.

"Some men like to rebuild cars," Saban once said. "I enjoy rebuilding football teams."

O.J. Simpson considered quitting football after being used as a decoy by Bills coach John Rauch. But he underwent a rebirth under Saban, who gave him the bodyguards and the carries necessary for him to realize his football potential.

"He was like an uncle you loved or hated," Simpson said in an April 1982 interview with *Inside Sports* magazine. "If he caught you out past curfew on a weekend, instead of making a big fuss, he'd say, 'Let me buy you a drink and let's talk,' and then you'd be quietly fined on Monday. He treated you like a man."

DID YOU KNOW...

That the Bills lost their first five games in 1962 under first-year head coach Lou Saban?

Anderson echoed those emotions. "Before Lou came [to Miami] I just wanted to be average, just another ballplayer," he said. "When I got tired or if anything hurt, just barely, I would walk off the field. Then he started getting on me and I said, 'I'm not getting paid for this.'

"Finally, one day during a film session he stopped and said, 'Turn on the lights.' He said, 'I was a fool to think you could be something. You have no heart, no guts. It's pathetic.' If I'd had a gun, I'd have hid somewhere and shot him, but then I began to realize I really did have a lot more to give. I began applying the discipline he gave me to my life and society."

Added Floyd Little, the former Syracuse University All-American and Denver Broncos All-Pro running back: "I wouldn't play for anyone for a million dollars now, but if Lou Saban asked, I'd play for nothing."

In the fall of 2006, New York Yankees owner George Steinbrenner honored his longtime friend by endowing a $300,000 National Football Foundation scholarship award in Saban's name. The two met for the first time while collaborating on a youth track-and-field program in Cleveland back in 1948. Seven years later, when Saban was the head football coach at Northwestern University, he hired Steinbrenner to be an assistant on his staff. The Yankees owner reciprocated by hiring Saban as a scout, consultant, and president of the Bronx Bombers nearly three decades later.

> "SOME MEN ENJOY REBUILDING CARS; I ENJOY REBUILDING FOOTBALL TEAMS."
> —COACH LOU SABAN

In announcing the honorary scholarship, Steinbrenner said: "Of all the athletes and people that I have coached and been involved with, Lou is the ultimate warrior, molder of men, and builder of teams. I learned under Lou the importance of discipline and loyalty. His pursuit of perfection transcends everything else. That's the best that you can say about a man."

That pursuit of perfection gave new meaning to the term "well-traveled."

FLAKES

Longtime coach and short-time general manager Marv Levy likes to talk about choosing players with good character. And through the years, the Bills have succeeded in identifying character—as well as characters. Some of their players, especially from the early years of the franchise, have been a little—how shall we say?—different. They've borne nicknames such as "Cookie" and "Pit Bull" and traveled to the beats of their own drummers.

Along the way, they contributed much more than touchdowns, tackles, and interceptions. Their off-the-field antics have added to the Bills' colorful history.

Here's a look at some of the flakier guys who have suited up for the team.

Cookie Gilchrist: The 6'2", 250-pound running back was one of the most talented and zaniest Bills of all time. A true freak of nature, Gilchrist had a 52-inch chest and a 32-inch waist and could run like a deer. He was so versatile that the Bills used him to kick field goals and extra points, and some believe he would have made an awesome linebacker. In fact, before one season, Cookie offered to play both ways if Ralph Wilson would double his salary. The Bills owner declined.

Like Ralph Kramden in the old television series *The Honeymooners*, Gilchrist always seemed to be involved in some get-rich-quick scheme. He once purchased land in Canada because he was told it contained a gold mine. "Turns out there wasn't any gold mine; there wasn't even any property," recalled Eddie Abramoski, the Bills' trainer for more than three decades. "The guy had sold him a bogus deed for some property that actually was sitting on the bottom of one of Canada's deepest lakes."

Cookie later ran his own maid service in Toronto. The advertising slogan on the side of his van read "Lookie, lookie, here comes Cookie." He soon went out of business.

> **DID YOU KNOW...**
>
> That with a .604 winning percentage, Wade Phillips ranks behind only Marv Levy among Bills head coaches?

Gilchrist also tried to make a quick buck by selling earmuffs bearing the Bills logo before the '64 championship game. But the Canadian resident failed to get a permit to bring the merchandise across the border and was left holding the bag once again.

"He couldn't get them cleared through customs until two days after the game," Abe said. "I can still see it now. Here's Cookie with 3,000 earmuffs in his garage. He couldn't even give them away."

The irrepressible Gilchrist's career with the Bills lasted just three seasons before he forced a trade to the Denver Broncos. He still ranks sixth on the team's all-time rushing list, with 3,056 yards, and ninth in scoring, with 248 points.

Tom Rychlec: Although he led the team in receiving in 1960 with 44 receptions for 581 yards, Rychlec was better known for his idiosyncrasies. "He was one strange dude," Abe said.

> ## "THERE USED TO BE A MOUSE IN FRED'S LOCKER, BUT IT MOVED OUT BECAUSE IT WAS TOO FILTHY IN THERE."
>
> —GUARD JIM RITCHER ON FRED SMERLAS'S MESSY CUBICLE

Rychlec would agree. He was known to bite the tops off Coke bottles and chew on the glass. He would also eat night crawlers he found on the practice field. But he was best known for his hookslides. He would run onto the practice field, slide into the goal post, and signal either "out" or "safe." "I guess you could say I wasn't playing with a full deck," Rychlec admitted in an interview years later. "But if you think about it, you have to be a little crazy to play this game anyway."

Henry Schmidt: He played only one season for the Bills, but that was long enough for him to earn a spot on the team's All-Flake Team. Schmidt actually lived in his car outside the old War Memorial Stadium during the 1965 season. "Guys didn't make much money playing ball back then, so Schmidt figured he could save a little cash that way," Abe said. "The bottom line was that he was cheap. He had a sleeping bag and blankets and he would take showers at the stadium and park his car in the tunnel when the weather started becoming cold and windy. That was a tough neighborhood around War Memorial, but Schmidt never worried about someone attacking him. He told me, 'Abe, nobody's going to bother somebody crazy enough to live in his car.' I have to admit it, he had a point."

George Saimes: One of the greatest Bills players. Also one of the strangest. The four-time All-AFL safety was always analyzing things to death. "He had 18 different pairs of football shoes, so he could make sure he had the right traction, depending on what field we were playing on," Abe said. "He'd change them several times a game, so we always had to make sure they were lined up and ready to go near the bench."

Saimes also did a lot of experimenting away from the field. "He ate sunflower seeds long before it became fashionable," Abe said. "And he used to mix motor oil with his shampoo because he had read it would help stop hair loss."

It didn't work, but that didn't stop him from conducting other experiments. After retiring, Saimes wound up becoming an NFL scout and had a successful post-playing career with the Washington Redskins.

Daryle Lamonica: He backed up Jack Kemp until 1967, when he was dealt to the Oakland Raiders in arguably the worst trade in Bills history. Nicknamed the "Mad Bomber" because he loved throwing deep, Lamonica was a headstrong quarterback who often locked horns with his equally headstrong coach, Lou Saban. "I remember one game Saban sent in a pass play, and Lamonica ran the ball instead and scored a touchdown," Abe said. "Lou went nuts on the sidelines, and Lamonica tried to calm him down by pointing out that he had scored on the play." Lou would have none of it. Afterward, Lou told reporters, "There are times when I think Daryle runs onto the field without his helmet on."

> **"HE WAS REGARDED AS A BUFFOON BY OUR PLAYERS AND HE HASN'T CHANGED, HE'S THE SAME NOW. HE CALLS HIMSELF 'THE COACH,' BUT A MORE APPROPRIATE TITLE WOULD BE 'TOKYO ROSE.'"**
>
> —MARV LEVY, TALKING ABOUT COACH-TURNED-RADIO-TALK-SHOW-HOST CHUCK DICKERSON'S INCESSANT CRITICISM

Birtho Arnold: Few Bills made a bigger impression than Birtho. He was so heavy he had to be weighed at the local feed store. The scale there had a limit of 375 pounds and legend has it that Arnold exceeded the limit. The big offensive lineman out of Ohio State was known to hide bags of potato chips in his dorm room—no wonder he could never make weight and get into shape. He was cut before the 1960 season opener.

Norman King: Another guy who didn't make the regular-season roster. King had a habit of breaking curfew. Legend has it

---

DID YOU KNOW...

That Joe Ferguson and Jim Kelly hold the team record for most fumbles in a career, with 76? Joe Cribbs owns the single-season mark with 16 in 1980, while replacement game quarterback Willie Totten set the single-game record with five against Indianapolis on October 4, 1987. Interestingly, Totten also fumbled four times the following week against the New England Patriots.

---

that he would shimmy down a drainpipe and head to a local watering hole, where he would play piano well into the night.

Mitch Frerotte: Known as "Pit Bull" because of his nasty demeanor, Frerotte rode Harleys on the back roads of western New York and listed "house cleaning" as one of his hobbies in the Bills media guide. He loved heading out on the highway with fellow offensive lineman Glenn Parker.

One time ESPN's Joe Theismann was in town to do a report, and he sat on Frerotte's motorcycle without permission. As Frerotte walked up the stadium tunnel following practice, he noticed from a distance that someone was on his Hog, and he went nuts. "If you value your life, you better get the f*ck off my bike in a hurry," Frerotte bellowed.

"I never saw Theismann move so fast," Bills special-teamer Steve Tasker recalled. "He looked like he had seen a ghost—or maybe Lawrence Taylor coming at him on a blitz."

TRADES, DRAFTS, AND FREE AGENTS

A BILL OF GOODS

At the Bills press conference announcing his promotion on December 30, 1985, the new general manager introduced himself as "Bill Who?" It worked because at the time, the only household in which Bill Polian was a household name was his own.

It didn't take long for this feisty Irishman to become known throughout western New York and the National Football League as the Frank Lloyd Wright of his profession. Thanks to his keen assessment of football personnel and his adroit handling of players' agents, Polian turned a laughingstock franchise into perennial Super Bowl participants. It was a remarkable metamorphosis considering that the Counterfeit Bills he inherited had won just four of 32 games during the '84 and '85 seasons.

Here's how this modern-day "Buffalo Bill" did it.

1. He hired Marv Levy to replace Hank Bullough midway through the 1986 season. Some accused Polian of cronyism because he had worked for Levy in Montreal, Kansas City, and Chicago. But if Polian was indeed doing a friend a favor, Levy paid him back in spades, guiding the Bills to an unprecedented four consecutive Super Bowl appearances and becoming the winningest coach in franchise history.

2. Polian signed Jim Kelly and several other United States Football League players who contributed mightily to Buffalo's stampede in the late '80s and early '90s. Kelly, of course, became

the most important piece of the puzzle because he gave the franchise instant credibility, providing the team with its first legitimate quarterback since Joe Ferguson in the early 1980s. But Polian also signed Pro Bowl center Kent Hull, linebacker Ray Bentley, kicker Scott Norwood, and reserve defensive back Dwight Drane after the USFL went the way of the Brontosaurus and Tyrannosaurus Rex.

3. He made *the* trade. On Halloween Day 1987, Polian sent two number one draft picks, a number two pick, and 1,000-yard rusher Greg Bell to Indianapolis in exchange for Cornelius Bennett, who blossomed into a Pro Bowl linebacker. The move enabled Shane Conlan to move to his natural position—inside linebacker—and took much of the double-team pressure off Bruce Smith, making the sack-happy Bills defensive end even more dangerous.

4. Polian oversaw some superb drafts. He had a role in the bountiful '85 crop, which yielded Smith, all-time Bills reception leader Andre Reed, and super-sub quarterback Frank Reich. His fingerprints were also all over the '87 draft, which yielded six starters—Conlan, cornerback Nate Odomes, fullback Jamie Mueller, defensive end Leon Seals, tight end Keith McKeller, and offensive tackle Howard Ballard. And, of course, who can forget the 1988 draft, in which the Bills selected their all-time leading rusher—Thurman Thomas—as well as starting nose tackle Jeff Wright and starting linebacker Carlton Bailey.

5. Polian revamped the front office, hiring astute judges of football talent such as John Butler, A.J. Smith, and Bob Ferguson.

Polian will be the first to tell you that Levy was an even bigger part of the team's success. When they first met about three decades ago, Levy was the general manager and coach of the Montreal Alouettes of the Canadian Football League. Polian was an aspiring football scout, scraping out a living selling advertising for an upstate New York farm journal.

Levy had asked his assistant, Bob Windisch, to line up some part-timers to scout NFL training camps. One of the people contacted was Polian. It was the start of an incredible relationship that saw Polian present Marv during Levy's induction into the Pro Football Hall of Fame in 2001.

"I didn't know Bill from Adam," Levy recalled. "But after reading his [scouting] reports, I wanted to get to know him. I remember saying to Bob, 'This stuff is so thorough, so meticulous, we need to hire the man who compiled these.'"

And so they did, thus beginning a close friendship between Levy and Polian.

"I wouldn't have achieved 1/100th of what I've achieved professionally without Marv Levy," says Polian, who has been voted NFL Executive of the Year five times by his peers and guided the 2006 Colts to the Super Bowl title. "Marv Levy gave me my start, and through the years, he gave me an education about football and about life."

Polian followed him from the Alouettes to Kansas City when Levy became head coach of the Chiefs in 1978. They went their separate ways after Levy was fired following the 1982 season, but were reunited two years later when Levy became coach of the Chicago Blitz of the United States Football League. After one season, Polian went to Buffalo, where he became director of scouting.

DID YOU KNOW...

That defensive tackle Ron McDole intercepted six passes while with the Bills, the most in franchise history by a defensive lineman?

The Bills were in a bad way when Polian first arrived. Under Kay Stephenson and Hank Bullough, they had lost 37 of their last 43 games, and midway through the 1986 season it was apparent that a coaching change was needed.

"We were 2–7 and it was obvious that the players just weren't responding to Hank; he had lost the team," Polian says. "I went to Ralph Wilson and said, 'Mr. Wilson, there's only one man I'd recommend to turn this around, and that man's name is Marv Levy.'

"I told him how Marv had rebuilt the program in Kansas City, but that the NFL players' strike came along and everything fell apart. Mr. Wilson called [Chiefs owner] Lamar Hunt, and Mr. Hunt told him that he had made a mistake firing Marv. That was good enough for Mr. Wilson, and the rest, as they say, is history."

That historic era included six division titles, four AFC championships, and an unprecedented four consecutive Super Bowl appearances.

Polian did his part by adding Pro Bowl players Thurman Thomas, Cornelius Bennett, and Shane Conlan to a roster that already included Jim Kelly, Bruce Smith, Andre Reed, Fred Smerlas, Kent Hull, and Darryl Talley. And Levy did his part by molding this group of talented, egotistical players into a championship team.

"Marv was a master psychologist," Polian said. "The team was pretty worn down by Hank, who was known for long practices and long meetings. So, in Marv's first meeting with the team, he spoke for about two minutes. He told them, 'Men, I only have three rules. Be on time, be prepared, and be good citizens. Now, let's go out there this Sunday and kick the Pittsburgh Steelers' butts.' The players gave him a standing ovation."

Though Polian left the Bills over a dispute with Wilson following the Bills' second Super Bowl appearance in 1992, he never lost contact with Levy.

"I still seek his counsel, and his influence on me continues to be profound," Polian said. "Just ask anybody in the Colts organization, and they'll probably tell you that they're sick and tired of hearing me tell stories about Marv. I'm always repeating his bromides, and, of course, his jokes."

That's only appropriate, because you can't tell either man's career story without mentioning the impact they had on each other.

DID YOU KNOW...

That Brian Moorman holds the Bills punting record with an 84-yard boot in a game against Green Bay on December 22, 2002? It was one of three punts he's boomed more than 70 yards during his career. In 2006, he set a club record with punts of 50 or more yards in 14 consecutive games.

THE HALLOWEEN HEIST

There were those who thought General Manager Bill Polian was mortgaging the Bills' future when he acquired Cornelius Bennett back on Halloween night in 1987. Yeah, the first-round pick out of Alabama was highly touted; some scouts had even billed him as the second coming of Lawrence Taylor.

But Bennett had yet to play a single down in the NFL, and the pages of the sports history books are filled with hyped rookies who never came close to living up to their potential.

By exchanging two first-round draft picks and running back Greg Bell, who had already logged a 1,000-yard season, for Bennett, Polian was like the poker player who was throwing everything into the pot. All or nothing. What you got?

As it turned out, the gamble paid off royally for Polian and the Bills. Bennett's career lived up to the hype. He became the final piece of the puzzle on defense, the pass-rushing linebacker who took blocking pressure off defensive end Bruce Smith and enabled Shane Conlan to move from outside linebacker to his more natural position on the inside.

And it also solidified Polian's reputation as one of the most astute wheeler-dealers in National Football League history.

"It was at that point that all the guys in the locker room began looking at Polian differently," said Bills special-teams great Steve Tasker. "We began to realize that this guy was a genius—and certainly not somebody you wanted to play poker against, because Bill was as shrewd as they came about knowing when to hold 'em and knowing when to fold 'em."

It takes years to fairly evaluate any trade, and time showed that with this one, the Bills got away with highway robbery.

Indy was only too happy to cut its losses and make the trade; Bennett had already sat out the first half of the season over a contract dispute, and it appeared that he was ready to follow through on his threat to sit out the entire season and reenter the draft. The Bills were reluctant to part with two first-round picks, but they didn't have a problem jettisoning Bell, who was regarded by some of the veterans as a prima donna.

General Manager Bill Polian landed pass-rushing specialist Cornelius Bennett on Halloween night 1987, and he was a frightful sight for the likes of New England quarterback Drew Bledsoe.

It didn't take Bennett long to start paying dividends. On his very first play as a pro—just a week after he arrived in Buffalo—Biscuit flushed Denver Broncos quarterback John Elway out of the pocket and batted down his pass.

"We were all like, 'Wow! Did you see that?'" Tasker recalled. "It was an incredibly athletic play, because Elway was the most mobile quarterback in the league at the time."

Bennett finished the game with a sack, two quarterback pressures, and three tackles in limited action that day. It would be an omen.

Bennett wound up earning five Pro Bowl invitations and finished his career as the Bills' third all-time leading sacker. He and Smith developed a friendly competition to see who could get to the quarterback first. Occasionally they arrived at the same time, sandwiching the signal-caller and usually forcing a turnover.

History shows that the Bills easily got the best of the deal. The Colts sent Bell and draft picks to the Rams in exchange for running back Eric Dickerson. Though Dickerson was destined for the Pro Football Hall of Fame, he was on the downside of his career by the time he wound up in Indy. Bell, meanwhile, turned in two more 1,000-yard seasons with the Rams, but faded rapidly after that. And none of the draft picks the Bills parted with amounted to anything in the NFL.

Polian's genius would also be evident in the drafts following his Halloween Heist. Despite not having a first-round draft pick in 1988, he was able to select Thurman Thomas in the second round—and all Thomas did was go on to become the all-time

DID YOU KNOW...

That the Bills have twice scored 117 points in a three-game stretch? The first occasion was during the 1964 season, when they strung together scores of 48, 35, and 34 points. The second time occurred in 2004, when they had 37, 38, and 42 in consecutive weeks. The record for most points against the Bills in a three-game stretch occurred in 1976, when they yielded 130.

leading ground-gainer in Bills history. In 1989, Polian was without a first- or second-rounder, but his third-round selection of wide receiver Don Beebe out of tiny Chadron State in Nebraska proved to be another master stroke. Beebe wound up being a speed-burner who stretched the defenses and took pressure off Andre Reed and James Lofton.

TRADE WINDS
The Best Trades in Bills History

1978: O.J. Simpson to the San Francisco 49ers for five draft choices. One of those picks was used to select Joe Cribbs, who wound up becoming the Bills' third all-time leading rusher. Another choice was used to select Tom Cousineau. He never signed with Buffalo, but that turned out to be a blessing in disguise—when the Bills traded Cousineau's rights to the Cleveland Browns, they acquired a first-round draft pick that they used to select Jim Kelly in 1983. Buffalo also cashed in one of the five Simpson picks to select Ken Johnson, who was a solid contributor at defensive end for several seasons. Juice, meanwhile, was in the twilight of his career when he was unloaded, so the Bills made out like bandits. Credit new coach Chuck Knox for having the foresight to pull the trigger on this one.

1987: Greg Bell and three high draft choices to the Indianapolis Colts for linebacker Cornelius Bennett. Sure, the Bills parted with an awful lot, but Biscuit wound up becoming one of the all-time Bills greats. A feared pass-rusher, he relieved some of the double-team pressure on defensive end Bruce Smith and allowed the Bills to move Shane Conlan from outside linebacker to his more natural position, inside linebacker.

1972: Wide receiver Marlin Briscoe to Miami for a first-round draft pick that general manager Bob Lustig used to select Pro Football Hall of Fame guard Joe DeLamielleure.

1976: Lustig dealt first-round bust Walt Patulski to the St. Louis Cardinals for a second-round pick. The Bills used that pick to draft Joe Devlin, who became a staple at left offensive tackle for more than a decade.

1977: Tight end Paul Seymour to the Pittsburgh Steelers for wide receiver Frank Lewis. Lewis still had plenty of gas left in the tank, putting together two 1,000-yard-plus receiving seasons. Seymour never played for the Steelers.

DID YOU KNOW...

That Bobby Moore was Ahmad Rashad's given name?

1960: Defensive tackle Al Crow to the Boston Patriots for running back Wray Carlton. Crow vanished from the scene, and Carlton ranks as the Bills' fifth all-time leading ground-gainer.

1974: Quarterback Dennis Shaw to the St. Louis Cardinals for wide receiver Ahmad Rashad. Shaw was on his way out of the NFL, and Rashad developed into one of the NFL's most dangerous receivers during his season with the Bills.

The Worst Trades in Bills History

1967: Quarterback Daryle Lamonica and receiver Glenn Bass to the Oakland Raiders for quarterback Tom Flores and receiver Art Powell. Ralph Wilson still has nightmares about this one: Lamonica took the Raiders to the Super Bowl in 1968. Flores was injury-prone and played only two seasons with the Bills, primarily as a backup. Powell, who once caught 16 touchdown passes in a season with the Raiders, was over the hill and lasted only one year in Buffalo.

1971: Defensive end Ron McDole to the Washington Redskins for draft choices used to select Bob Kampa, Jeff Yeates, and John Ford. The Bills mistakenly thought McDole was through, but the big lineman known as the "Dancing Bear" wound up having eight quality seasons with the Redskins' "Over-the-Hill Gang" and was named to their all-time team. Kampa, Yeates, and Ford vanished from the scene.

1998: A first-round pick to the Jacksonville Jaguars for backup quarterback Rob Johnson. General Manager John Butler was one of the lead architects of the Bills' Super Bowl run, but even he would have admitted he blew this one. The athletically gifted quarterback was sack-prone and never fulfilled the potential Butler and the Bills' scouts had envisioned.

STANDING PAT

Sometimes the best deals are the ones you don't make. In early January 1970, Bills owner Ralph Wilson offered to trade O.J. Simpson to the Los Angeles Rams in exchange for quarterback Roman Gabriel. Simpson had struggled through an injury-shortened rookie season, and Wilson figured the former Heisman Trophy–winning running back from the University of Southern California would be happier playing for a West Coast team.

The Rams, though, wanted nothing to do with the deal. Gabriel was an established NFL quarterback, a rare commodity, while Simpson was a young player who had not shown many signs of fulfilling his enormous potential. Plus, O.J. was viewed by some as damaged goods, since he was coming off a knee injury.

So the deal was never consummated, which turned out to be a blessing for the Bills. Simpson's pro football career finally began to take off in his third season with the arrival of Head Coach Lou Saban and precocious offensive linemen Joe DeLamielleure and Reggie McKenzie.

Gabriel wound up having a solid career; the Juice wound up having a Hall of Fame career.

1980: Joe DeLamielleure to Cleveland for the Browns' second-round draft pick in 1981 and their third-round selection in 1982. Buffalo used the '81 pick on LSU defensive end Chris Williams and traded the '82 pick to Seattle for guard Tom Lynch. Neither player did much with the Bills. DeLamielleure wound up having several more productive seasons with the Browns before ending his career back in Buffalo.

In the Bills' defense, DeLamielleure had a strained relationship with Coach Chuck Knox and essentially left the team with no choice but to trade him. In retrospect, Joe D probably wished he had never forced the issue—he considered himself a diehard Bill and would have wanted to spend his entire career with the team.

1997: A third-round pick to Oakland in exchange for backup quarterback Billy Joe Hobert. Although he was 0–5 as a spot-starter in three seasons with the Raiders, Bills scouts thought Hobert was a diamond in the rough. One of Buffalo's talent assessors even compared him to Jim Kelly. More like Jim Carrey.

When Hobert finally got a chance to play after Todd Collins was injured, he bombed badly. The Monday after a loss to New England, he told the media he hadn't studied much leading up to the game. That didn't sit well with his coaches and teammates, and he was jettisoned a few days later.

THE BEST AND WORST DRAFTS IN BILLS HISTORY
Blue Chips

1979: Funny how things work out. The first Bills pick was Tom Cousineau. He snubbed Buffalo for the Canadian Football League, and the fans were all over Ralph Wilson for being a tightwad. In retrospect, not signing Cousineau turned out to be one of the best things to happen to the Bills.

Buffalo eventually traded the rights to Cousineau in exchange for a first-round pick, which it used to select Jim Kelly in 1983. But even if the Bills had received nothing for Cousineau (who, by the way, turned out to be a big bust), this still would have ranked as Buffalo's best draft. Norm Pollom's scouting department discovered seven starters in this crop: Fred Smerlas, a five-time Pro Bowl selection at nose tackle; Jerry Butler, a wide receiver who became the seventh most prolific pass-catcher in team history; Jim Haslett, a linebacker who led the team in tackles five times; offensive tackle Jon Borchardt; defensive tackle Ken Johnson; safety Jeff Nixon; and safety Rod Kush.

> "COACHES TREAT US LIKE CARS. THE OLD ONE IS WORKING FINE, BUT THEY WANT A NEW ONE ANYWAY. THEY THINK THEY'LL ENJOY IT MORE."
>
> —BILLS KICKER JOHN LEYPOLDT

1985: This one laid the foundation for the Bills' revival and Super Bowl run. It yielded the greatest sacker in NFL history, Bruce Smith, the most prolific pass-catcher in Bills history, Andre Reed, as well as two other starters—cornerback Derrick Burroughs

CALIFORNIA DREAMIN'

Sid Gillman was considered one of the most innovative thinkers in football history, a genius when it came to the passing game. But the former San Diego Chargers coach outsmarted himself when he tried to sneak Jack Kemp through waivers back in 1962. The quarterback was out with a broken middle finger on his passing hand, so Gillman figured no one would want to take a chance on damaged goods.

He figured wrong, because the instant Bills owner Ralph Wilson saw that Kemp was available, he claimed him off the waiver wire. It cost Buffalo $100—the best $100 Wilson ever spent.

The quarterback paid immediate dividends, helping the Bills recover from an 0–5 start to finish 7–6–1. They made the playoffs the next year and then won back-to-back AFL titles, with Kemp winning league MVP honors in 1965. He finished with more passing yards than any quarterback in AFL history, with 21,130.

and wide receiver Chris Burkett—and two important backups—quarterback Frank Reich and linebacker Hal Garner.

1987: Another kick-butt draft with six players who became starters: linebacker Shane Conlan, cornerback Nate Odomes, tight end Keith McKeller, defensive end Leon Seals, offensive tackle Howard Ballard, and fullback Jamie Mueller.

1961: The Bills discovered three of the best offensive linemen in team history in this draft: Pro Football Hall of Fame guard Billy Shaw, five-time AFL All-Star tackle Stew Barber, and center Al Bemiller, who was named to the Bills' Silver Anniversary team in 1984.

Buffalo Chips

1966: The first three picks were Mike Dennis, Jim Lindsey, and Randy Jackson. Never heard of them? That's understandable. None of them ever played for the team, ending up with other NFL squads.

1975: Roland Hooks, a tenth-rounder, was the only pick to distinguish himself. That's how bad this crop was.

1965: Jim Davidson in the first round, nobody in the second, and Alan Atkinson in the third. Need we say more? Atkinson never played for the Bills and ended up starting for the Jets' Super Bowl team.

1982: This will forever be remembered as the Perry Tuttle draft. Pollom wanted the Bills to choose wide receiver Mike Quick, but Coach Chuck Knox was insistent on selecting Clemson's Tuttle, the nation's top-rated receiver. So the Bills took Tuttle, who played a couple forgettable seasons before being released and winding up in the Canadian Football League. The Philadelphia Eagles got "stuck" with Quick, who made the Pro Bowl five seasons in a row.

FIRST-ROUND DRAFT PICKS
Striking Gold

- 1969: O.J. Simpson. After a slow start, the Juice went on to a Hall of Fame career.
- 1973: Joe DeLamielleure. He started as a rookie and became the best blocker on the best offensive line in football.
- 1980: Jim Ritcher. He was a center at North Carolina State, but switched to guard and went on to play 203 games for the Bills, third most in team history.
- 1983: Jim Kelly. After shunning the Bills to play two seasons in the USFL, he arrived in Buffalo and established himself as the greatest quarterback in team history.
- 1985: Bruce Smith. Some wanted the Bills to choose Doug Flutie instead, but Buffalo wisely opted instead for the defensive end who became the NFL's all-time sack leader.

DID YOU KNOW...

That Rob Johnson was the most accurate passer in Bills history, with a 60.5 completion percentage to go along with a 2.56 interception percentage? Sadly, he never became the quarterback many believed he could be.

- 1986: Will Wolford. This offensive left tackle started as a rookie and helped lead the Bills to three Super Bowls before bolting for the free-agent bucks.
- 1987: Shane Conlan. The Penn State star turned in six stellar seasons as a run-stuffing linebacker.
- 1991: Henry Jones. He turned in nine solid seasons as a starter at strong safety.
- 1995: Ruben Brown. The guard from Pitt went to eight Pro Bowls, most ever by a Bills offensive lineman.
- 1996: Eric Moulds. He established himself as one of the NFL's top wideouts and the second most prolific receiver in Bills history.

Striking Out

- 1970: Al Cowlings. O.J.'s wheelman in the white Bronco spent three nondescript seasons as a defensive lineman with Buffalo.
- 1972: Walt Patulski. Arguably the biggest draft bust in team history. The defensive end from Notre Dame was the first overall pick of the draft and was expected to be the second coming of Deacon Jones. He spent four mediocre seasons with the Bills.
- 1974: Reuben Gant. He played seven seasons in Buffalo, but the tight end known derisively as "Old Stone Hands" and "Reuben Can't" dropped almost as many passes as he caught.
- 1975: Tom Rudd. The linebacker held out most of his first training camp in a contract dispute and was gone after the '77 season.
- 1977: Phil Dokes. This defensive end retired from the NFL after just two seasons.

DID YOU KNOW...

That, in a strange coincidence, all-time Bills greats Thurman Thomas and Andre Reed finished their careers in Buffalo with 87 touchdowns apiece?

- 1978: Terry Miller. The running back had a decent rookie season, but went downhill in a hurry and was gone by 1980.
- 1979: Tom Cousineau. The number one overall pick never played a down for the Bills. He went to the Canadian Football League, and the Bills traded his rights to Cleveland to get the first-round pick they used to draft Kelly in 1983.
- 1981: Booker Moore. Several months after being drafted, the Penn State running back was diagnosed with Guillain-Barré syndrome, an illness that leads to chronic muscle weakness. He rushed for a total of 420 yards in four seasons with the Bills.
- 1982: Perry Tuttle. Believed to be a can't-miss wide receiver, Tuttle caught just 24 passes in two years with the Bills and was out of the NFL by 1985.
- 1983: Tony Hunter. The tight end from Notre Dame was actually chosen ahead of Kelly and linebacker Darryl Talley. After two average seasons, he was dealt to Los Angeles in exchange for quarterback Vince Ferragamo.
- 1986: Ronnie Harmon. His time in Buffalo will best be remembered for that dropped pass in that playoff game in Cleveland.
- 1990: James Williams. He was a cornerback who couldn't cover and couldn't catch.
- 2000: Erik Flowers. Too light to play defensive end in the pros, Flowers was jettisoned by the Bills after just two seasons.
- 2002: Mike Williams. The big offensive tackle from Texas was the fourth overall pick of the draft, but lacked the toughness and drive to become a dominating player. He stands out as the biggest draft failure of the Tom Donahoe era.

Some Other Free Agent Acquisitions of Note

- Steve Tasker: Marv Levy's first personnel decision was a good one. He claimed Tasker off waivers from Houston, and the little guy wound up becoming the greatest special-teams player in the history of the game.
- Kent Hull: This was another great move by Polian. Signed after the USFL folded, the center became the quarterback of the Bills' offensive line for more than a decade.

- Steve Christie: Signed away from Tampa Bay, Christie replaced Scott Norwood and became the most prolific scorer in Bills history.
- James Lofton: He was supposed to be washed up, but he wound up scoring 21 touchdowns and earning a Pro Bowl berth in three seasons with the Bills.
- Bryce Paup: He recorded 17.5 sacks in his first season with the Bills (1995) and earned Pro Bowl honors all three years he was with the team.
- Ted Washington: This massive nose tackle was the clogger of several highly rated Bills defenses in the late 1990s. He made the Pro Bowl three times in his last four seasons with the team.
- Kenneth Davis: He proved to be a great backup for Thurman Thomas at running back during the Super Bowl years.
- Doug Flutie. Signed out of the Canadian Football League, Flutie had some magical moments, particularly in 1998 when he earned Pro Bowl honors and had a cereal named for him.

DID YOU KNOW...

That the Bills were a combined minus-34 on the take-away, give-away list during their back-to-back AFL championship seasons in the mid-1960s?
